The Executive Guide to Integrated Talent Management

The Executive Guide to Integrated Talent Management

Kevin Oakes and Pat Galagan, Editors

Foreword by Tom Rath

Alexandria, Virginia

ASTD Press is an internationally renowned source of insightful and practical information on workplace learning and performance topics, including training basics, evaluation and return on investment, instructional systems development, e-learning, leadership, and career development.

Ordering information: Books published by ASTD Press can be purchased by visiting ASTD's website at store.astd.org or by calling 800.628.2783 or 703.683.8100.

Library of Congress Control Number: 2010941375

ISBN-10: 1-56286-754-7
ISBN-13: 978-1-56286-754-6

ASTD Press Editorial Staff:
Director: Anthony Allen
Manager, ASTD Press: Larry Fox
Project Manager, Content Acquisition: Justin Brusino
Senior Associate Editor: Tora Estep
Associate Editor: Ashley McDonald
Editorial Assistant: Stephanie Castellano
Copyeditors: Alfred Imhoff
Indexer: Abella Publishing Services, LLC
Proofreader: Abella Publishing Services, LLC
Interior Design and Production: PerfecType, Nashville, TN
Cover Design: Ana Ilieva Foreman
Printed by Versa Press, Inc., East Peoria, IL, www.versapress.com

Contents

Contents

Section VIII: Pulling It All Together

Foreword

Tom Rath

Most workers are not engaged in their jobs. The vast majority of people Gallup studied (80 percent) can't even give a strong "yes" when asked "Do you like what you do each day?" (Rath and Harter, 2010).

What's even more troubling is that organizations, on average, are not helping to improve this situation. Instead, they bring new people in and allow their engagement to *decrease* substantially as each year goes by. As leaders, we have no choice but to fight this downward spiral toward disengagement. If we do nothing, employees will tune out, give less effort, and eventually leave. Or worse yet, they will stay around for a decade and erode the engagement of their peers and customers.

Finding a solution to this challenge is a central focus of this book. In the chapters that follow, you will hear from the best minds in the field of talent management as they describe how to build stronger organizations. This unique book brings together well-known academics, experts, and practitioners from some of the most admired institutions in the world. While breaking down long-held institutional barriers, these thought leaders reveal how you can engage your people from recruitment to retirement.

Each day when an employee shows up at work, he has the liberty to exhibit as much—or as little—effort as he wants. As we have all witnessed, two different people can walk into an office, spend the exact same number of hours on a task, and achieve dramatically different outcomes and levels of productivity. While each employee has a distinct set of talents that must fit a job role to begin with, once a person has been hired, a great deal of the responsibility for engaging that worker rests within the control of one person: his manager.

Despite the direct return on such investment, employers continue to focus far too little energy on the development of managers and leaders. One of the most important findings from decades of Gallup's workplace research is that people leave bad managers and local teams—not companies. And the more we explore the relationship between an employee's engagement and his physical health, the more we realize that the quality of his manager might be as important for his health as the quality of his doctor. Yet the majority of workers do not have a good relationship with their boss.

Time-use studies reveal what people do with their time, who they spend it with, and how they feel at various points throughout the day (Kahneman, et al., 2004). What's most striking from this research is that the person we *least* enjoy being around is our boss (Krueger, et al., 2008). Of all the categories people ranked, from friends to relatives to coworkers to children, they rated the time they spent with their manager as being the worst time of the day. Even when compared to a list of specific daily activities, time spent with the boss was rated lower than time spent doing chores and cleaning the house. This may help explain why people who have worked for a bad manager could be at much greater risk for cardiovascular disease (Nyberg et al., 2009). Bad management may literally be as detrimental as bad medicine.

To bring this to life, think back to when you were in grade school sitting through a class in which you had very little interest. More than two-thirds of workers around the world experience a similar feeling by the end of a typical workday. To explore why so many people are disengaged at work, we recruited 168 employees and studied their engagement, heart rate, stress levels, and various emotions throughout the day. Before the study began, we collected data about each employee's level of engagement (Rath and Harter, 2010).

As part of the experiment, the participants carried a handheld device that alerted them at various points in the day when we would ask them what they were doing, who they were with, and several other questions about their mood. We also asked each participant to wear a small heart rate monitor. We collected saliva samples to gauge stress levels throughout the day (via the stress hormone cortisol). The cortisol levels provided a direct physiological measure of stress levels at various points each day.

After reviewing all of these data, it was clear that when people who are engaged in their jobs show up for work, they have an *entirely different experience* than those who are disengaged. For those who were engaged, happiness and interest throughout the day were significantly higher. Conversely, stress levels were substantially higher for those who were disengaged. Perhaps most strikingly, disengaged workers' stress levels decreased and their happiness increased only toward the end of the workday.

It appears that managers who are simply not paying attention create much of this disengagement. If a manager ignores an employee, there is a 40 percent chance that the employee will be actively disengaged. If a manager is at least paying attention—even if he focuses on the employee's weaknesses—the chances of that employee being actively disengaged go down to 22 percent. But if a manager primarily focuses on an employee's strengths, the chance of that employee being actively disengaged is just 1 percent, or 1 in 100 (Rath, 2007).

Fortunately, this means that the engagement and productivity of almost any workforce is within our control as we develop strategies to help people learn, lead, manage, and develop talent. Ensuring that our organization's leadership and talent management initiatives pay attention to and develop people every day should eliminate barriers, silos, and disengagement. As the chapters that follow will detail, one of the central aims of integrated talent management is to create an organization-wide plan to meet these challenges.

Recruiting, compensation, reward, performance management, succession planning, engagement, retention, and leadership development must all be thought of holistically. Each of these components is critical to the ability of an organization to learn, grow, and thrive. Learning professionals are in a unique position to help the organization bring these elements together where it matters most: to all employees as they figure out how to maximize their contribution to the organization's goals and mission.

However, it is also clear that professionals in learning, HR, organizational development, and talent management cannot go it alone. We need to marshal the resources of local managers and leaders to create real cultural change. As we provide these key leaders with the learning and integration they need, this is how we can have an impact that spans far beyond the number of people our efforts reach directly.

Solving the challenges presented in this book is a high-stakes game. If an organization fails to integrate its approach to talent management, it will experience decreases in productivity, quality, and customer engagement. If an organization takes initiative and confronts these challenges, it will create engagement, profits, and stronger workplaces.

References

Kahneman, D., A.B. Krueger, D. Schkade, N. Schwarz, and A.A. Stone. (2004). "Toward National Well-being Accounts." *The American Economic Review, 94*(2), 429–434.

Krueger, A.B., D. Kahneman, D. Schkade, N. Schwarz, and A.A. Stone. (2008). *National Time Accounting: The Currency of Life (Working Papers No. 1061)*. Princeton, NJ: Princeton University, Department of Economics, Industrial Relations Section.

Nyberg, A., L. Alfredsson, T. Theorell, H. Westerlund, J. Vahtera, and M. Kivimaki. (2009). "Managerial Leadership and Ischaemic Heart Disease among Employees: The Swedish WOLF Study." *Occupational and Environmental Medicine, 66*(1), 51–55.

Rath, T. (2007). *StrengthsFinder 2.0*. New York: Gallup Press

Rath, T. & Harter, J. (2010). *Wellbeing: The Five Essential Elements*. New York: Gallup Press.

About the Author

Tom Rath is a leading business thinker and one of the bestselling authors of the last decade. His first book, *How Full Is Your Bucket?*, was a number one *New York Times* bestseller. Rath's book, *StrengthsFinder 2.0*, is a long-running number one *Wall Street Journal* bestseller. His most recent *New York Times* bestsellers are *Strengths Based Leadership* and *Wellbeing: The Five Essential Elements*. In total, Rath's books have sold more than three million copies and have made more than 250 appearances on *The Wall Street Journal* bestseller list. Rath currently leads Gallup's workplace consulting business. In this role, he guides the organization's practices and research on employee engagement, selection, strengths-based development, leadership, and wellbeing. Rath also serves on the board of VHL.org, an organization dedicated to cancer research and patient support. He earned degrees from the University of Michigan and the University of Pennsylvania. Tom and his wife, Ashley, and their two children, live in Washington, D.C.

Acknowledgments

Obviously, this book wouldn't exist without the generous contributions from the world-renowned thought leaders and experienced practitioners who contributed chapters. They not only lent us their time; they lent us their considerable expertise and valued opinions. For these, we offer our sincerest thanks to the wonderful authors who created the pages you are about to read.

We would also like to thank several others who contributed to this book:

- ASTD, for making this book possible and continuing to further the strategic impact of the learning profession.
- The staff at i4cp and the research staff at ASTD, whose excellent research into all aspects of human capital and high performance organizations augments the book's contents.
- The members of ASTD's Integrated Talent Management Advisory Committee, who have supported this effort since the beginning:
  - Susan Burnett, Yahoo
  - Rick Coffey, Boeing
  - Debbie Eshelman, SENSA Solutions
  - Jeanette Harrison (chair), Learning Consultant
  - Leslie Joyce, Novelis
  - Edward Lawler III, University of Southern California
  - Annmarie Neal, Cisco

— Kevin Oakes, i4cp

— Deb Wheelock, Mercer.

We're proud of this book, but even prouder of what it represents for the profession: effectively integrating and managing talent improves organizational effectiveness. As Dave Ulrich—called the most influential person in HR—succinctly points out in chapter 17, "Talent differentiates, drives productivity, determines customer service, and increases intangible shareholder value. Talent matters. Talent is too important to be left to uncoordinated events."

Whether leading an orchestra or an employee base, the *coordination* of talent—synergistically maximizing each player's unique but complementary skills and competencies—is the key to success. We hope this book helps every talent conductor create virtuoso performances worthy of frequent standing ovations.

Introduction: Too Many Soloists, Not Enough Music

Kevin Oakes and Pat Galagan

The term "talent management" is such an enigma. In an industry like learning and development that consistently reinvents its vocabulary, never before has a human resources term garnered so much attention and yet been so misunderstood and overly hyped—and, by some, overly scorned. Ironically, given the many articles, books, presentations, and rhetorical efforts that have been devoted to it over the years, talent management remains a mystery to most.

So why did we decide to add to this proliferation with this book? Our years of observing and opining about the learning and development industry led to growing puzzlement and some persistent questions related to talent management:

- How does organizational talent become a capability?

- Why do so many otherwise exemplary companies continue to acquire, develop, and deploy their talent with isolated practices that, if put together and coordinated, could become so much more effective?

- Why do so many leaders proclaim that people are their most important asset but then not manage this asset from a unified perspective?

- Why do organizations go to so much trouble to acquire the best talent, only to keep those soloists in private studios and never assemble the orchestra for virtuoso performances?

Our perspective comes from observation, research, and conversations over many years. Our two organizations—the Institute for Corporate Productivity (i4cp) and ASTD—have collected data through multiple studies of how companies acquire their talent, how they develop it and manage it, and what works and what doesn't. Between us, we've had conversations with thousands of people whose professional lives center on the effort to make organizations perform better through their people.

Often there is understandable logic to the way companies approach the acquisition and development of talent today, but typically it's an approach built on the avoidance of pain—the pain of breaking familiar patterns and doing things differently. So whole industries behave this way, following rigid and outmoded practices like these:

- the five-year plan
- the selection of people with high potential by some calcified numerical formula
- succession planning that ignores the reality of a mobile workforce
- recruiting in a vacuum
- development divorced from strategic direction.

You probably have your own list of talent-related practices that no longer make sense in a fast-moving world.

Abolishing Silos

Herein lies the real puzzle. Although many companies know that talent matters for growth as well as survival, managing it as a coherent strategy is still very rare. Despite all the attention paid to the idea of talent and its management—remember the "war for talent" breaking out nearly 15 years ago?—the practices surrounding it are largely unchanged. In many companies, even several with dedicated talent officers, talent management is still regarded as just another term for succession planning and executive development. And though research clearly shows that functions such as performance management are most easily integrated with learning and development, why do so few companies actually integrate them?

We've seen too many companies whose talent management practices continue to be stuck in silos—a metaphor, we like to point out, from the agricultural era. In today's knowledge worker era, these silos, all under the umbrella of HR, often have their own agendas, compete with each other for available budget, and actively work against each other to gain political power. We believe that this too-common reality in companies is not only immature but also unproductive. True integration is long overdue and deeply necessary. Even the talent management pundits and zealots will secretly admit that there are too few examples of companies that are actively and successfully integrating the silos. For practical ideas on how to do this, see the sidebar.

Slicing Through the Silos With Software
By Kevin Oakes

Almost a decade ago, the overly anxious CEO of an HR technology company began pitching to me the idea of merging his company with my company to form the ultimate entity: a complete talent management suite. At the time, I was CEO and chairman of Click2learn, a leading learning management company (I would later merge Click2learn with Docent to create SumTotal Systems). The landscape of human capital technological solutions was still very nascent, but the idea of a suite of applications that would address all aspects of HR had, for a few years, already been envisioned by many in the learning and development industry.

This particular CEO was not the first to approach me with the idea of joining forces, but he was easily the most aggressive. His pitch: "Together, we can be the only provider to offer end-to-end HR and learning products and services in the attain–train–retain continuum. LET'S SEIZE THIS OPPORTUNITY NOW, AND DRIVE THE MARKET!!!" is the way he ended one memorable email.

The problem, as I unconvincingly kept describing to him, was that the potential buyers in corporations are in silos. Very few—if any—companies at the time were positioned organizationally to take advantage of such a holistic solution. Almost all firms ran their HR groups separately. Their recruiting people couldn't have cared less about their performance management people—who

---

often fought for budget with their learning and development people—who were typically not even in the same building as the compensation and benefits group. In short, we could preach all we wanted, but there was no one congregation ready to hear our message.

Today, the landscape has changed. Though the preaching has only increased in volume over the years, companies now are much more prepared to take advantage of the fully integrated talent management technology suite. And technology providers finally are ready to deliver, primarily because of what that aggressive CEO wanted in the first place: the merging of complementary companies. You probably remember some of the names: DigitalThink, Thinq, Pathlore, GeoLearning, Learn.com, Centra, Interwise, Softscape, RecruitForce, Resumix, Hire.com, BrassRing, Vurv, Salary.com. You and I could list hundreds more. The obvious commonality among these companies, of course, is that they all were purchased. But their maybe-not-so-obvious similarity is that they all, arguably, were considered "point solutions," addressing and excelling at only a small portion of the talent management life cycle. Today's mergers-and-acquisitions activity is all about seeking the holy grail of the fully integrated talent management suite, a quest that no vendor—despite the propaganda—has yet to fully achieve. But that's quickly changing.

The talent management field is maturing both technically and in helping corporations realize how to use integrated talent management for their strategic benefit. However, the term "talent management" is still thrown around too loosely by suppliers. It's no wonder that buyers get confused. As this book goes to print, I've just returned from an investor conference featuring several human capital vendors. Almost every single CEO and chief financial officer talked about their firm's strength in "talent management." I witnessed the CEOs of two staffing companies say they were "leaders in talent management." Their definition obviously differs from ours in this book.

Although mergers in general help achieve the technical functionality needed, the benefits of a merger often take much longer to take effect than projections claim. The truth is that most firms tend to be strongest at their roots. Thus, not only are vendors more technically capable with their original products, but it's also how they *think*. If you are a hammer, everything looks like a nail, so most firms continue to approach the market from the mindset that helped them succeed in the first place.

Although this situation is an understandable and natural fact of this talent evolution, buyers need to be prepared for it as they begin to adopt the integrated talent management suite. There will be strengths, and there will be weaknesses, and many will be based on the heritage of the vendor. The "complete suite" is unlikely to be truly complete for some time, and as a result, many companies will continue to integrate multiple vendors' products to achieve the functionality they need.

This evolving integration, whether between vendors or within one vendor's complementary applications, typically centers on mapping data between human capital functions. And the data most in demand are the skills and competencies of the workforce.

A common refrain from corporate practitioners is, why can't I centrally store the skills of job applicants when they are hired, and pass those to the performance function along with the skills deficits that we identified, and they in turn pass data on to the learning function, which ties into the compensation function? Up until recently, the answer was *lack of data integration*—both among the technology platforms and modules currently on the market and among the HR functions.

Integration continues to be the primary challenge in the learning and development industry, according to a study conducted by ASTD in cooperation with i4cp. Only 19 percent of the respondents said that their companies integrated talent management components to a high or very high extent, and only one in five said their firm has the technological capability to do so. Though capabilities keep getting added, the easiest prediction to make is that integration will continue to be an issue for years to come.

However, when it comes to integration, the same study found that the two components integrated the most in successful implementations were the learning and development function and performance management. This is the easiest place to begin in many companies, because these functions naturally go hand in hand, and several providers of technological solutions focused on this link early in the development of their integrated suites. Identifying performance issues, and recommending learning and development opportunities that address those issues, is a hallmark of good performance management, but it's amazing how many companies don't do this today. In the future, it's easy to envision these two functions never being separated, but today it's still rare to see them completely integrated. Other core elements that are germane to top integrated talent management programs include leadership and high-potential development, retention, and engagement.

Although the integration of talent management poses many challenges, it's important to point out the core strategies that organizations can follow to improve their chances of success in integrating:

- Make the whole executive team, rather than just a single
HR leader, responsible for talent management, and ensure

that leaders see talent management as a vital element of the organizational culture. This is easier said than done, of course, but companies that are successful at talent management typically have their most senior team not only involved but also held accountable.

- Ensure that your organization's talent management processes are coordinated before implementing technological solutions. If your organizational design is poor, if there is little synergy and sharing among groups, and if there is no flow of information in the employee life cycle, automating these processes will only compound the chaos.

- When selecting technological solutions, proceed with intelligent skepticism. It's a given that all features of a solutions suite will rarely work exactly as advertised, but small issues are often fixable—it's sharing data across all functions that is most worrisome. As a result, many buyers start with one or two components instead of the entire suite. When selecting components, think down the road and pick a vendor that you expect will be able to support you with additional core components in the future. And even though you may not use everything from the start, make sure you do a thorough test drive of all integrated components and talk with as many other earlier buyers as you can to gain an understanding of possible pitfalls.

- Finally, measure talent management, and make sure that these measurements are aligned with your business goals. The field of talent management metrics and analytics is growing, and it's clear that the best companies not only measure relentlessly but also focus primarily on quality and effectiveness metrics instead of efficiency.

Advances in software as a service, cloud computing, and an increased understanding of data mapping are helping to make the integration of talent management easier and are allowing companies to see the light at the end of the tunnel when they will be able to take full advantage of the integrated talent management suite. This, according to our research, will benefit the bottom line of corporations by leveraging internal talent more strategically. Although the learning and development industry will never be at a loss for preachers willing to deliver this particular sermon, there's obviously still much missionary work left to do.

Yet despite the generally sad state of talent management, the landscape is slowly changing. In our recent work, we have come across several corporate practitioners and industry experts who have success stories to share—sometimes small, sometimes revolutionary—which frankly are what encouraged us to create this book.

However, we started this project with an admitted bias: From our research and observations, it is clear to us that the learning and development function has a critical role to play in integration. We firmly believe that all the traditional HR silos can and should be integrated on some level with learning and development. Therefore, we explicitly invited the contributors to this book to reflect our perspective. Most actually did. By and large, the authors of the chapters that follow highlight how a particular silo or HR function is integrated into the whole of talent management and how it utilizes learning and development to be more strategic and productive for the organization.

Definitions Abound

It's amazing that today, more than a decade since the term "talent management" was introduced, nearly everything spoken or written about it still starts with a definition. Many of these definitions, including some that we've written, are so comprehensive that they verge on being incomprehensible. Though this may be a symptom of a practice undergoing growing pains, it has only added to the confusion. The upshot is that most organizations don't have an agreed-on definition of talent management (see figure 1-1).

Most of the definitional issue centers on which HR components are to be included in integrated talent management. And this is one part of the confusion that makes sense. Not every organization has the same kinds of talent challenges. Some need frequent fresh supplies of frontline workers who are quickly ready to serve customers. Others need seasoned engineers who can innovate in highly competitive, technical fields. Many need versatile global talent who can develop into the leaders of the future. And all need their talent to turn on a dime when events such as deep recessions and market upheavals change the rules of the game.

Figure 1-1. Most Organizations Don't Have an Agreed-On Definition of Talent Management

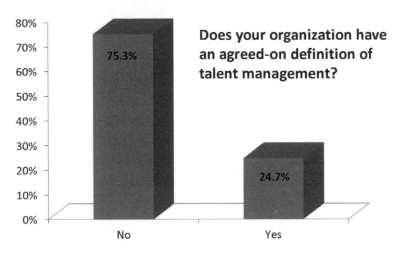

Source: Data collected by the Institute for Corporate Productivity and ASTD.

On the basis of our research into the various human capital functions that reside in companies today, we identified six key components of talent management:

- recruiting
- compensation and rewards
- performance management
- succession management
- engagement and retention
- leadership development.

We organized this book so that each of these components constitutes one section containing two or three chapters addressing important aspects of the topic. Yet though these six topics are the major practice areas that corporations typically cite as making up their integrated talent management strategies, that doesn't mean they are the only ones for your organization.

In chapter 2, Wharton professor Peter Cappelli provides a logical way to think about what components of talent management to emphasize. You'll note that his choice of components differs somewhat from ours. Let that be fair warning: This is not a book of rules. It's a collection of viewpoints and working practices described from two angles—the thought leader's and the senior practitioner's. Accordingly, the first chapter in each section reflects on research-based theory informed by many years of observation and thought, and the second (and in one case third) chapter describes practices under way in large, successful enterprises.

A Menu, Not a Recipe

As you pursue integrated talent management in your organization, when deciding which components to emphasize, your obvious choices will be the functions that will most quickly put the right talent in the right jobs at the right time. So it won't matter if your effort is "disproportionately" focused on top executives, or key scientific jobs, or super sales generators—as long as it makes strategic sense and supports your key business goals.

Moreover, despite our bias for integrating the role of learning and development, we aren't campaigning for the primacy of one component over another. In the chapters that follow, you'll see from the practitioners' accounts that while finding, developing, and keeping talent are common to all the companies featured in the book, most emphasize one component over another for reasons that make good business sense to them.

At 3M, for instance, where innovation is the lifeblood of the organization, there's a strong focus on engaging people and encouraging them to stretch (see chapter 13). At Edwards Lifesciences, where CEO Michael Mussallem drives a culture of execution and accountability, talent management focuses strongly on succession planning, to put at least two candidates in line for every key job (chapter 11). And at GE, the überincubator of leadership development in our time, the emphasis is on "judgment capacity" arrived at through industry-leading practices such as leaders teaching leaders and action learning (chapter 15). From Hertz's focus on rewarding knowledge transfer (chapter 7), to Cisco's linkage of performance plans to the CEO's vision (chapter 9), to Agilent's embracing of evidence-based HR (chapter 3), this book is full of both practical examples and strategic viewpoints for today's corporations.

Although similarities abound, every company is unique. Therefore, we're not strict constructionists when it comes to processes, as long as you have one for stitching things together around the common goal of better performance. And that's really what this book is about: *achieving higher organizational performance and workforce productivity through optimized talent management.*

Every chapter describes a talent management process in both theory and practice for the component it covers. And the authors address how to integrate these processes with other talent management efforts in other parts of the organization:

- linking skills uncovered in the recruiting process to the succession planning process

- leveraging compensation plans to create a pay-for-performance culture

- enabling greater employee engagement for greater corporate innovation and less unwanted attrition.

Thus, the authors of the following chapters reveal what is working for their high performance organizations, and how others can adopt these practices. We invite you to join the conversation.

Section I

■ ■ ■

An Overview of Integrated Talent Management

Managing Talent in a Changing Landscape

Peter Cappelli

Getting the right people with the right skills into the right jobs—a common definition of talent management—is the basic people management challenge in any organization. Though talent management often focuses on managerial and executive positions, the issues involved apply to all jobs. Among the major subtasks within the talent management function are the following:

- workforce planning, which estimates future demand

- hiring (entry-level and lateral) and internal development and promotion, which are the "make-versus-buy" options for meeting demand

- succession planning, which brings the planning process down to the individual level.

Failures in talent management may be more recognizable than the concept itself. These failures include mismatches between supply and demand—on the one hand, having too many employees, leading to layoffs and restructurings; and on the other hand, having too little talent or not being able to find the skills that are needed. These mismatches are among the biggest challenges that employers face. During the past decade, many employers have lurched from surpluses of talent to short-falls and back again. These lurches are incredibly costly to organizations, although it is fair to say that most internal accounting systems are not yet sophisticated enough to be able to capture all those costs. (In general, it is easier to measure the costs of having too many workers than not enough or the wrong kind, as those costs spill over to the business.)

Before the Great Recession that started in 2008, most talent management practices in the United States fell into two equally dysfunctional camps. The first and most common was to do nothing—making no attempt to anticipate needs and developing no plans for addressing them. Data from a recent survey by the Society for Human Resource Management suggest that about two-thirds of all U.S. employers are in this category (Fegley, 2006). Making no attempt to anticipate and plan for needs in practice means that employers are relying on outside hiring to meet their needs. The downsides of this approach became more apparent as more competitors turned to it, making it harder and harder to find good candidates outside the organization. The second strategy, which was common among older companies, relies on complex bureaucratic models of forecasting and succession planning from the 1950s—legacy systems that grew up in an era when business was highly predictable. These models fail now because they are inaccurate and unresponsive, along with being costly in the face of uncertainty.

The current recession has halted most efforts to innovate in talent management. Many employers have learned from the recession that it is now important to make even fewer long-term commitments to employees in case the need to cut back returns. This has included investments in developing employees. Contracting, temporary help, and other contingent solutions have grown in importance as we have begun to pull out of the worst of the recession.

But these lessons are merely what not to do, and we have taken them about as far as they can go. It is hard to imagine that talent management can progress if we simply give up on the problem and essentially try to outsource it to the market, hoping talent needs can be met by outside hiring or contracting.

New Ways to Think About Talent Management

A number of new tools are now available to make talent management decisions easier. Most of these are software based, and for the most part, they automate tasks that were performed with paper and pencil: tracking employee performance gaps, tracking development experiences, making matches with training programs, and so on. Real progress can happen by making some tasks easier. We all know, for example, that it was possible to record TV shows decades ago using early VCRs, but it was so difficult to do that few people bothered. New technology such as TiVo has made it so much easier to record shows that it has changed how people watch TV. Making it easier to perform the separate tasks within talent management means at a minimum that they will more likely be done more efficiently.

Nevertheless, real innovations are less likely to come from these tools than from different ways of thinking about the basic challenge. The first step in a new approach is to be clear about the goal. Talent management is not an end in itself. The goal of talent management is the more general task of helping the organization achieve its overall objectives. In the business world, this objective is to make money. And making money requires that you understand the costs along with the benefits associated with your talent management choices. Governments and nonprofit organizations have an analogous concern: to maximize efficiency in the talent management process.

Helping an organization achieve its goals begins with recognizing that the most important problem facing virtually all employers is the need to respond quickly to changes in competitive environments. Employers now change strategies, structures, and operations quickly and repeatedly in response to customer demands, competitor innovations, regulatory changes, and other outside factors. Though these changes may be more pronounced in the for-profit world, governments and nonprofits also experience their own sea changes now on a regular basis. The developments driving these responses are difficult to predict, and mistakes in responding—waiting too long to change or planning for circumstances that fail to pan out—are costly.

In this context, the basic problem for organizations is to manage *risk*, which we can think of as the costs associated with events that are uncertain or at least difficult to predict. Business risk, driven by uncertainty about business demands, translates directly into risk for talent management.

Many of the most innovative models for managing talent come from outside the United States, especially from countries such as India and Singapore, where frequent and chronic talent shortages make problems in talent management easier to see and more pressing. The common attribute in these models is that they take costs and benefits seriously, including the costs of risk, and they rely on data to assess how they are doing. And much of the work on these models has been done by people from fields outside human resources—especially engineers—who thus have no prior legacy models to constrain their thinking. How some of these ideas might be applied to the subtasks within talent management is explored in the following pages.

Workforce Planning

Workforce planning in the past has been synonymous with forecasting. The problem is that business forecasts essentially don't work. The business environment is so uncertain that long-term forecasts are essentially worthless, and useful predictions are likely to be limited to short-term estimates based on real-time data: What customers are buying today is used to predict what they will buy next week.

The alternative to workforce planning is to recognize that the future is uncertain and try to assess what this uncertainty looks like. Scenario planning is useful in this regard, as are simulations that allow the parties to look for "robust" conclusions or estimates that are similar, even when important assumptions change.

Other techniques for making progress include borrowing lessons from supply chain management, such as minimizing the costs of being wrong in our forecasts (that is, is it worse to have too much or too little talent in our context?) and adjusting our forecasts accordingly (see Cappelli, 2009).

Cheaper Development

Another task that is central to improvements in talent management focuses on the development side. How can we recoup investments in employees when the need for their skills is uncertain in the long run and they can walk out the door, taking those skills with them? Better forecasts of skill needs certainly help in this regard, as do improvements in retention, although the latter often come with their own costs.

An alternative way to deal with the problem of recouping investments in development is to focus on reducing development costs. There is a great deal of interest in cheaper training systems, especially online and distributed training programs. But the problem with skills has more to do with work-based competencies. Here an alternative is to get employees to share the costs of development. Employees are now the main beneficiaries of investments in their development because of their ability to cash them in on the open market. The simplest way in which individuals contribute to the costs of their own development is by voluntarily taking on learning projects, perhaps in addition to their normal work.

Assuming that the candidates are more or less contributing their usual performance in their regular jobs and that their pay hasn't increased, they are essentially doing these development projects for free. Some employers now offer promising employees the opportunity to volunteer for projects with leadership teams, sometimes restricting them to projects outside their current functional area to broaden their experience. The employees get access to company leaders, a broadening experience, and good professional contacts—all of which will surely pay off later. But they pay for these benefits by contributing work of value to the employer. Similarly, tuition reimbursement programs, in which employers pay college tuition and employees attend classes on their own time, offer additional ways to share the investment in development.

The most important approach to developing employees focuses more on the benefits than the cost side: to increase the value of employee contributions by speeding the process that gets them to jobs that add greater value to the organization. This approach requires that you spot talent and potential early and then give the employees opportunities to advance faster than they otherwise might. Many companies are moving away from the difficult task of attempting to predict who is ready for which new job and moving toward a self-nomination model. The best of these provide opportunities to literally let an employee try out a role and see how they do. If you want to see who can lead a team, there is nothing better than giving various people the chance to try leading it. Finding opportunities like these, in which candidates can fail quickly and cheaply, is a key element of developing talent and an important task for line managers in the talent management process.

Alternatives to Succession Planning

Succession planning—the effort to predict vacancies, especially in executive roles, identify candidates to fill those vacancies, and then prepare them for succession—is arguably the biggest waste of time in the talent management portfolio of tasks. It is the focus of top executive attention, not only because it affects their careers but also because it is crucial to company success. It has been a remarkably underresearched topic, in part because of the difficulty in getting information on outcomes associated with different practices (Cappelli, 2010). But what we know about the practice of succession planning suggests that the process needs considerable improvement: Few organizations do it at all, and those that do rarely have evidence of success.

When you think about it, the reasons for this poor track record are obvious. Succession plans assume away uncertainty because they are based on the idea that we know which jobs will need to be filled in the future, what those jobs will require, and which current employees will be around to fill them. Many companies update their succession plans every year to try to keep up with the fact that jobs change and individuals leave. As a practical matter, how useful is a plan if it must be changed every year? What problem is it solving? Anecdotal evidence suggests that when these plans exist, they are actually used about one in four times. The most common outcome is for leaders to conclude that the plans do not reflect the current reality and to abandon them.

A better approach is to take uncertainty as given and find ways to manage it vis-à-vis questions of succession. One well-known approach is to use the principle of portfolios or talent pools, where one avoids trying to develop employees to fit narrow, specialized jobs. Instead, a group of employees is developed with broad and general competencies that should fit into a range of jobs. Once the candidates are developed, they are allocated to actual vacancies, as opposed to trying to guess years in advance where vacancies will occur and which individuals should slot into them. The fit between candidate and specific job may be less than perfect, but more just-in-time training and coaching can help close the gap. And this imperfect fit is a smaller problem than dealing with the likely risks of using traditional succession planning techniques—of promising an advancement that does not materialize or of having no one who fits the changing demands of jobs.

New Career Paths

Making matches between individuals and jobs is the process through which individual employees acquire the work-based skills necessary for purposeful career advancement. Making these matches used to be the most important task performed by the executives and managers in charge of talent management. These *chess masters*, as they were called, moved candidates around the business equivalent of a chessboard—the organization chart. If an employee refused to take a new position or a transfer, his or her career advancement stopped.

This chess master model ran into trouble when labor markets tightened because good candidates could easily say no and get a job somewhere else. To improve retention, virtually all companies—96 percent in a recent private survey of companies by the recruiting firm Taleo (www .taleo.com)—have moved away from this model to internal job boards, where employees apply for new positions inside the organization. If employees want new jobs, employers concluded, we should at least make it easier for them to find them within the organization.

This process effectively takes the problem of managing one's career and turns it over to employees. Although there are many benefits to this new approach, one drawback for employers is that they have much less control over their internal talent. Programs that attempt to mitigate this risk by negotiating a balance between the employee's and the employer's interests in career advancement are one of the truly new developments in talent management.

Some of these efforts involve simply providing information about career paths—that is, descriptions of how individuals have advanced in the past. Others go much further, attempting to negotiate compromises between the preferences of the organization and those of the employee. It is fair to say, however, that most organizations have not yet thought through how to handle the challenge of managing a more open internal market for talent. Whether employers are willing to let it become a real market, where internal hiring managers are allowed to compete for internal talent by raising wages or making their jobs more attractive, is an open question.

Managing Talent in the Future

The new way of managing talent described here takes organizational goals and not human resource targets as its starting point. Its purpose is to help the organization perform, and it does this by managing the talent risks that are generated by uncertainty in business demand and the new, more open labor markets. This new approach to talent management may help resuscitate the process of developing managerial talent, which risks being choked off because employers cannot envision how to do it in the current environment. And this lack of a process for developing talent internally increases the demand for outside hiring, which in turn causes retention problems elsewhere. This further undercuts the ability to develop talent internally and creates a vicious circle that erodes managerial talent.

To address these uncertainty-driven problems will require two different basic approaches:

- First, giving greater priority to the goals of talent management, in part by recognizing the value of doing it right versus the costs of doing it wrong.

■ And second, pursuing greater integration of talent management and related practices across the organization and with each other.

It is useful to keep these overall approaches in mind as you delve into the details of the various aspects of talent management in the rest of this book.

References

Cappelli, Peter. 2009. "A Supply Chain Approach to Workforce Planning." *Organizational Dynamics,* January–March, 8–15.

———. 2010. "Succession Planning." In *APA Handbook of Industrial and Organizational Psychology*, edited by Sheldon Zedeck. Washington, DC: American Psychological Association.

Fegley, S. 2006. *Succession Planning: A Survey Report.* Alexandria, VA: Society for Human Resources Management.

About the Author

Peter Cappelli is George W. Taylor Professor of Management and director of the Center for Human Resources at the Wharton School of the University of Pennsylvania. He is also a research associate at the National Bureau of Economic Research, served as senior adviser on employment policy to the Kingdom of Bahrain from 2003 to 2005, and since 2007 has been a Distinguished Scholar of the Ministry of Manpower in Singapore. Previously, he was a staff member on the U.S. Secretary of Labor's Commission on Workforce Quality and Labor Market Efficiency and co-director of the U.S. Department of Education's National Center on the Educational Quality of the Workforce. His recent books include *Talent on Demand: Managing Talent in an Age of Uncertainty* (Harvard Business Press, 2008), which was named a best business book for 2008 by Booz Allen; *The India Way: How India's Top Business Leaders*

Are Revolutionizing Management (with Harbir Singh, Jitendra Singh, and Michael Useem; Harvard Business Press, 2010); and *Managing the Older Worker: How to Prepare for the New Organizational Order* (with Bill Novelli; Harvard Business Press, 2010). He received degrees in industrial relations from Cornell University and in labor economics from Oxford University, where he was a Fulbright Scholar.

10 Essential Talent Management Lessons I Learned From My CEO

Teresa Roche

"We write to taste life twice, in the moment and in retrospection."

Anaïs Nin

I think I am a heretic.

Or perhaps I am onto something that does make sense, and I have my CEO and my manager to thank.

When asked to write this chapter, I was honored, humbled, and deeply concerned. A kaleidoscope of thoughts and feelings emerged, with a key one being that we do not say "integrated talent management" at Agilent. At least, the words are not spoken aloud.

And yet I absolutely know it is happening at Agilent.

I am the vice president and chief learning officer, and in this role, I am the lead architect and portfolio manager for the company's leadership development solutions, which have been at the center of talent management at Agilent.

There was a moment several years ago when I let go of my fixation on needing to see or hear the words "talent management" so that I could simply see what was occurring, much of which my team helped to make happen in partnership with our colleagues in human resources and our line leaders, beginning with our CEO, Bill Sullivan. Bill cares deeply about having the best talent at Agilent. There is not a business strategy where talent is not considered. I've known how much talent matters to Bill since I first met him in the early 1980s.

What follows are 10 talent management lessons I have learned from Bill over the course of my career at Agilent. (In fact, I am still learning some of them.) Keep these lessons in mind as you journey through this book. Take only the lessons that fit the conditions of your organization and the characteristics of your CEO.

Lesson 1: Understand the Criteria Used to Make Decisions

I used to come back from external peer conversations full of ideas and processes that, if applied, would guarantee we had an integrated talent management system. I somehow had convinced myself that applying others' work would cause magic at Agilent. Had I allowed myself to stay in this place of unrealistic expectations, I would have missed the moment to actually do something that had meaning and impact for the organization I was serving. What I now find personally valuable when I listen to others is to understand the criteria used for decisions made and the principles applied.

Lesson 2: Look for the Pull and Know What to Push

When Bill Sullivan became CEO in March 2005, he changed the strategic intent of Agilent from a diversified technology portfolio company to a single focus on measurement. One of his top three priorities was to have a best-in-class leadership team capable of delivering results and transforming the culture. Talk about an opportunity! Our very smart senior vice president of human resources, Jean Halloran, asked me to work with Bill and his team to define what leading at Agilent meant. After a series of key conversations, we have a clean and simple leadership framework that has guided us well for the past five years. It is written in words that others can easily understand and act on, and that has made this simple document alive in our company. The three dimensions are set and align strategy, build organizational capability, and deliver results; and underneath are specific behaviors.

Behind the scenes, we developed specific competencies for our Agilent leadership framework, and we scaled them appropriately to each level of leadership. Over time, we integrated them into our management practices and human resources systems from selection to performance management and total rewards. Not all at once, but when the pull for the work was present, we knew what program or practice to push next.

Lesson 3: Make It Part of the Work

At Agilent, a litmus test for us is whether the integrated talent management solution we provide delivers the results required in the Agilent dashboard. If it is a distraction, we go back to the drawing board. Everything we do needs to be embedded in the business requirements, and nothing can stand alone.

This simple phrase requires incredibly heavy lifting to ensure, for example, that we optimize development with programs that feature integrated, business-focused, applied learning. Or that the effectiveness of our performance management at Agilent is not about the completion of a form by a certain date, but that ongoing dialogue occurs between managers and employees about what is expected, how it is going, and what development is needed to get the work done.

Lesson 4: Start at the Top to Prepare the Soil for What You Need to Grow

After defining what leadership meant at Agilent, Bill said we needed to begin with our general managers. Most of me understood the merit of his words, and yet my head and heart were simultaneously screaming that we needed to do something for everybody. What others call talent segmentation, Bill simply saw as common sense and the only way to move the company forward. He assured me that if the general managers were clear on what was expected of them in terms of results and the specific leadership behaviors and values that define our company, these same managers would "beg" me to do the same for their next level of leaders. After five years, we are living the truth of his advice as we have thematically cascaded what we do only when we know that each leadership level is aligned before moving to the next.

Lesson 5: Principles Need to Be Consistent; Practices Do Not

A long-held bias came to light that development was the only path to building the right team. On our leadership framework we had "develop self and others" under "build organizational capability" and in Bill's second year as CEO, we added an additional leadership behavior, "create winning teams." What I came to realize is that leadership supply requires a hybrid approach of targeted recruiting, development, succession planning, and deployment. Often it is a one-size-fits-one approach with multiple strategies being done in parallel depending on what the business needs. Principles need to be consistent; practices do not. An example of this at Agilent is when we embark upon a growth initiative or enter an emerging market: We apply the same principle of ensuring the right talent at the right time, but the choice of practice fits the uniqueness of the specific situation—promote from within, hire externally, or redeploy talent.

Lesson 6: Measure What Matters

At Agilent, our approach to measurement is "outside in, inside out." Each year, we establish annual targets in the Agilent four-quadrant dashboard for customers, employees, leadership and culture, financials, and markets. We set our targets against external benchmarks.

The intention of the employees, leadership, and culture quadrant is to ensure we have best-in-class leadership as measured by our employees on a set of leadership practices, which provides the inside-out perspective. We then evaluate our scores against the top quartile of the external normative data provided by our leadership audit partner. The questions we ask relate to the specific leadership practices that drive our strategy and culture, and we choose practices that, when done well, pull other aspects of leadership to be effective. Twice a year, we ask questions— always fewer than 12, as we want to be truly focused on what really matters—and until we know we have embedded a specific leadership practice consistently, we keep at it. Presently the questions relate to customer orientation, speed and decisiveness, risk taking, and engagement, which together comprise our leadership brand of "speed to opportunity."

We are signaling the importance of leadership by aligning leadership metrics with other critical indicators of business performance. Similar to how we rolled out our leadership curriculum, we cascaded the individual audit reports starting first with the executives, then senior managers, followed by middle managers, and just this year, first-level managers received a report.

Lesson 7: Outputs Matter More Than Inputs

Outputs tell you if a true impact is occurring. In our performance-based culture, where clear objectives are set and aligned and leaders work in partnership with their employees, allowing appropriate levels of freedom to deliver results they are accountable for, things happen. Our leaders know that how they manage talent matters, and it starts with our CEO. Bill "walks" his way into his leadership, and if I look at what he does tacitly, I see the inputs and the outputs, but they are not what other seemingly high-performing companies do. For him, a talent review calendar with scheduled events such as talent discussions is not required if leaders know that building organizational capability is an expectation of their day-to-day work and, when done well, delivers the expected results.

Lesson 7 does not mean inputs have no value. Let me share two that really count. The first is "facts are our friends," and the second is the theoretical content that each of us should have to do this work. I believe that our field stands on the threshold of a critical intersection between economics and behavioral and cognitive sciences. Evidence-based human resources, such as the use of human capital analytics coupled with tried and true theories that we know and those that are emerging in the field of neurosciences, is where we bring value to the conversation. However, remember there is no need to remind people by saying the words that this is what you are doing. It is language only those of us in the field admire.

Lesson 8: Read the Wave—Monitor Your Environment and Adjust Your Plans as Needed

As a learning and development professional, you see things systemically. But just because you see the whole picture doesn't mean you won't miss signals. I have learned discernment from my CEO, who intuitively phases in changes. When we are in the middle of one, what next needs to be done is often revealed. Agility and adaptability are vital skills. Change is always coming, whether because of technology or demographic shifts or the economy; versatility is a currency worth having to stay competitive and ensure that the right talent is doing the right thing at the right time. Continually monitor your environment for changes and adjust your talent management plans accordingly. Bill often says it is one's second decision that matters more than the first decision. Your first causes you to act, but your second decision is the one you make to adjust if you find you are off track. Real impact comes from knowing when you are off and how to get back on to achieve a result. It is all about the art of correction as the true source of credibility.

Lesson 9: Conversations Matter

The only real process that matters is conversation. Mickey Connolly, co-author of *Communication Catalyst*, helped me see that all our work really happens in conversation. It requires being present to what is being said and remembering that when you have to convince someone, you have probably engaged them too late. In the face of resistance, stepping back and doing research by asking questions and listening is like remembering to hold hands in kindergarten when crossing the street.

Mickey told me to listen deeply for what people stand for that makes them speak against something. In one pivotal meeting with Bill, he was in complete disagreement about something that I presented, and I could not quite grasp why, but I remembered Mickey's words. That moment of consciousness and my conversation with Bill allowed me to learn that he was not so much *against* the HR team doing something as he was *for* managers owning the accountability for leadership. Over many years of such conversations with Bill, I have come to learn that in the marrow of his bones, he believes managers own leading their people. Little of my time is spent convincing leaders to care about leading. I have to deliver effectively what they really need to do so.

Lesson 10: Live the Change

This lesson is really the foundation of all the others. We have to be the change we seek. This requires knowing oneself and being "in integrity" with that which we teach and tell others. How I show up matters, and it is where I have grown the most in learning what integrated talent management is all about and *how to make it happen*. It is not seeing the words on a slide or hearing the words spoken that tells me it is present and happening. It requires paying attention to signals and outputs such as determining if you have the powerful signal of leaders participating in your programs both as presenters and/or participants and if the output of your post-performance actions after each development program indicates transfer and application has occurred for specific business results.

I recently shared our journey with others, and it was delightful to talk about the results we have achieved as a company since Bill become CEO. We have met the goals in each of the quadrants in our dashboard, even during the most significant economic slowdown ever experienced in our industry.

I am grateful to have a manager who supports me, my worldwide team that makes all of our work possible, and numerous colleagues I partner with daily at Agilent. I also know how fortunate I am to have a CEO who is willing to be taught but, more important, teaches me about talent management day in and day out.

About the Author

 **Teresa Roche** is vice president and chief learning officer at Agilent Technologies. Previously, she was vice president of human resources at Grass Valley Group and served in several executive human resources positions at Hewlett-Packard. She has a PhD in educational technology, a master's degree in counseling and personnel services, and a bachelor's degree in education and interpersonal and public communications, all from Purdue University. She co-authored the chapter "Application and Results: The New Finish Line for Managing at Agilent" in the book *Leading the Global Workforce: Best Practices from Linkage, Inc.* (Jossey-Bass, 2005) and the article "Innovation in Learning: Agilent Technologies Thinks Outside the Box," which appeared in the August 2005 *Journal of Organizational Excellence.*

Section II

■ ■ ■

Recruiting

Integrating Talent Acquisition to Dramatically Improve Business Impact

John Sullivan

When it comes to managing the capability and capacity of the work-force, organizations really only have three choices for augmenting their current state: Build talent in house, buy it from the labor market, or borrow it from others. The latter two options are the domain of talent acquisition (even though most talent acquisition leaders refuse to accept responsibility for total contingent labor management), and the first option is dependent upon an organization's ability to recruit talent that can be developed, so it is safe to say that talent acquisition is a key talent management activity.

In business, just like in sports, if you are responsible for bringing in innovators, superstars, and game changers, your impact can and should be clearly demonstrated. To maximize the impact of talent acquisition, organizations must make sure that talent acquisition operates smoothly as an integrated component of the overall talent management effort. Unfortunately, in most organizations, talent acquisition is not integrated and instead is overly siloed and operates autonomously. The isolation produces pervasive weaknesses in how organizations engage talent throughout the employee–service provider life cycle and results in staggering salary waste.

The Isolation of the Talent Acquisition Department

It's not enough to acknowledge that for decades HR departments have operated in silos and that for quite some time there has been a need for more integration. To remedy this problem, we first need to identify the root causes of this departmental isolation. My research and experience have led me to believe that one of the primary causes is that talent acquisition professionals differ from many other professionals in talent management. Successful recruiters are often very aggressive, competitive self-starters who work on projects that historically have been structured as independent activities. Talent acquisition also operates in a competitive environment where external entities are challenging them every day. Their isolation is compounded when other talent management professionals view talent acquisition activities as alternatives to their talent augmentation solutions and establish barriers to integration.

Talent acquisition leaders who have successfully overcome these issues generally began by identifying and acknowledging them. They then helped the organization understand how each departmental activity, when coordinated at a greater level, could produce more benefit than optimizing each independently.

The Negative Consequences of Isolation

Before turning our attention to talent acquisition, it's helpful to identify problems that occur when any business activity is not integrated. Business functions such as supply chain management and quality control have led the way in demonstrating the real cost of poor integration. Thanks to efforts in those areas, most executives today understand that when any interdependent function is too isolated or siloed, it can dramatically affect the output of an entire process. Just like a steel chain, a process is only as strong as its weakest link.

The primary consequences of poor integration are

- *Delay in process cycle time:* The lack of coordination between departments that touch the life cycle of the process can cause significant delays in workflow.

- *Increase in error rates:* As work flows through many disparate processes, there is a greater chance that steps will be omitted, or that transactions will get lost, resulting in a dramatic increase in costly errors.

- *Mass duplication of effort:* When departments do not coordinate well and rely on similar sets of data, there is a significant risk that the resulting processes will duplicate effort.

- *Limited process improvement or innovation:* Isolation can limit the sharing of best practices and information about opportunities, trends, and common problems.

- *Lack of accountability:* When departments operate in silos, internal customers may be confused about who is responsible or may be forced to shop around for solutions. It is also highly likely that performance metrics will be limited in scope to low-value transactional activities, limiting visibility into the full scope of positive/negative business impact.

In the case of talent acquisition, the effects can be direct or they can indirectly increase the workload of other talent management functions. For example, any weakness in coordination and integration throughout the process will directly affect the quality of recruits and new hires. A low quality of hires can certainly affect the image of the recruiting function, but it can also diminish organizational success.

Low-quality hires may not only produce poorer quality work, but they may also bring fewer innovations and new ideas to the organization. In addition, a series of bad handoffs between talent acquisition and other talent management functions responsible for helping new hires become productive more quickly (relocation, onboarding, training) may result in significant delays in the time needed to achieve minimum productivity.

Workload effects that result from improved integration include a decrease in the demand for performance management and training aimed at helping below-average performers reach minimum performance standards, a larger talent pool for promotions and leadership development, and an opportunity for the training and development function to focus more on capability building.

How Do You Determine Where to Integrate?

Talent management leaders should utilize these four criteria when choosing activities that require greater degrees of integration:

- The degree of activity interdependence, or the extent to which the success of one function relies on the actions of another. Using this criterion, you must determine to what extent an error or delay in one process directly affects the work or the results of another.

- Whether there is either a direct handoff of work or a direct sharing of information between two interrelated functions.

- The potential dollar loss resulting from work errors or delays attributed to talent problems.

- The existence of a gate that can stop progression through a linear process.

Six Levels of Working Together

There are different levels of working together, all of which may be utilized by an organization pursuing integrated talent management:

- *Shared communication:* having protocols in place that call for the regular sharing of information pertaining to issues relevant to multiple parties.

- *Defined cooperation:* creating a formal agreement between two parties to help each other, share information, provide services, and measure performance.

- *Close coordination:* reengineering department activities, processes, policies, and timelines to eliminate conflicts between departments and support cross-departmental objectives.

- *Synchronization:* mapping touch points between cross-departmental activities and establishing triggers so that processes directly coincide with or follow related activities.

- *Integration:* establishing a formally documented relationship between departments that maintains some degree of departmental autonomy but that establishes shared goals, joint decision making, integrated planning, process coordination/synchronization, and clear accountability.

- *Merger:* two or more once disparate departments uniting under a single leader and a newly developed organizational model and governance structure. Though rare, this is becoming more common in organizations with workforces that must maintain credentials—for example, healthcare and finance.

Determining what level of working together is appropriate is generally decided with a simple agreement among functional leaders. However, if you wanted to utilize criteria for that decision, two that you should consider include (1) the degree of interrelatedness (the extent that an error in one function affects the success of another) and (2) the average cost of an error caused from a lack of integration. In practice, coordination and integration are the most commonly selected levels of working together between recruiting and other major talent management functions.

Integrating Talent Management With Talent Acquisition

There is no uniform guidance on what talent management activities need to be coordinated with talent acquisition for an effort to be successful. However, early adopters of integrated talent management typically agree that direct and indirect relationships with talent acquisition are a great place to start. Let's consider each one very briefly.

Direct Relationships

The key direct relationships generally involve

- *Compensation:* Coordination is required with compensation to ensure that job descriptions remain consistent with market trends and that the salary ranges developed are validated against real-time data. Greater coordination is needed during the offer process to ensure that deadlines are met and that offers are presented in a manner that most improves the probability of acceptance.

- *Onboarding:* Nothing can delay the time needed to achieve minimum productivity more than an independent onboarding process that isn't triggered immediately upon hire. Improved coordination can result in a process that identifies the strengths and weaknesses of the current recruiting process and immediately solicits referrals from new hires.

- *Relocation:* When the relocation function operates independently, it's important that the relocation process trigger immediately upon acceptance of an offer.

- *New hire training:* similar to onboarding, having new hires who lack the necessary training contributes significantly to delays in the time needed to achieve minimum productivity. Greater coordination is needed to determine the hire-and-train target, that is, whether to hire a more junior employee and develop him or her or to hire an employee who is proficient from the start and to continue to adjust projected training needs based on labor market conditions.

- *Global recruiting:* Although it was once common for international recruiting to operate independently of home country recruiting, changing labor market conditions today require full integration or merging of efforts.

Indirect Relationships

The key indirect relationships generally involve

- *Leadership development, internal placement, and succession:* All organizations must continuously make build, buy, or borrow decisions regarding talent. Whatever the organizational model, functions charged with these activities must be integrated to ensure that decisions are accurate and nonpolitical.

- *Workforce planning:* In early adopters of integrated talent management, the role of workforce planning has changed. While workforce planning used to be about projecting gaps, today it is quickly becoming more about measuring the ability of the current talent management approach to close projected gaps and enable business strategy. Accomplishing this requires that workforce planners model all existing talent management activities, something that requires cooperation at the very least.

- *Performance management:* Performance management should notify recruiting well in advance of a new opening that is likely to occur as a result of an upcoming performance management action.

- *Offboarding:* Recruiting must coordinate with the offboarding/ exit process to ensure that data are shared on why recent hires are leaving, so that the recruiting process can be improved. In addition, exits pointing to systemic organizational issues may need to address organizational design or accepted management practice. When a corporate alumni or boomerang rehiring program exists, greater degrees of cooperation are needed to ensure that individuals who once delivered exceptional performance to the organization are periodically encouraged to return.

- *Retention:* It's important that the retention department communicate with recruiting, so that sourcing can develop talent pools and pipelines in advance for jobs that have high current and projected turnover rates. Without greater cooperation between talent acquisition and retention efforts, it is impossible to determine whether a retention or recruiting solution would produce a better return-on-investment for the organization.

■ *The innovation function:* For organizations with a structured innovation process, it's important that coordination occurs with talent sourcing activities so that individuals with a greater potential to deliver innovation successfully can be sought out.

■ *Merger-and-acquisition teams:* Because recruiting is familiar with external labor markets and candidate assessment, it can help with the postmerger process of determining which individuals should be retained. It can also help with premerger activities to assess the market value of a target's workforce.

■ *Shared skills functions:* Talent acquisition faces significant down time during periods of slow growth. As a result, the talent acquisition department needs to identify and work with other business functions where recruiters and their skill sets might be able to immediately contribute on temporary reassignment during slack periods. Typically, these functions include sales, customer service, high-potential assessment, and redeployment.

Actions for Improving Integration

Once talent management leaders decide which activities should be more closely integrated with recruiting, the next step is to develop an integration plan. Obviously, the task of integration is a little less complex in smaller, more centralized organizations, but whether your organization is big or small, the action steps to consider are still quite similar.

First, select an integration team and appoint a strong leader skilled in navigating organizational politics. Next, have the team develop the criteria that it will use to identify where and how a better relationship is needed between two currently disparate or poorly coordinated activities. Deliver the need specifications to the leaders of the two activities and allow them and their teams to devise how best to deliver their respective services in a manner that meets the new specifications. If there is general agreement between activity leaders, then the initial team should be dissolved. However, if there is conflict, the initial team will be needed to weigh arguments and settle disputes. Whichever team moves forward, its first actions should include identifying potential problems, putting together a business case that supports integration, and benchmarking integration best practices both inside and outside the organization.

The team should also identify which integration approaches or tools it will use to build cohesion between the two functions. Some of the most basic innovation approaches include shared correspondence, holding periodic joint meetings, and developing common goals. The next level includes sharing databases, joint training, shared goals, and rotating team members between the departments. The most sophisticated integration approaches include utilizing common metrics, a best practice sharing process, shared budgets, and making both individual and team bonuses dependent on the success of both functions. The integration team should also identify potential resistance and develop metrics for measuring the success of the overall integration effort.

Anticipate Resistance

Although dozens of benefits can accrue from closer integration, it is important to remember that even beneficial change within organizations will face resistance. Parties defending the status quo (often meaning their previous work product) can slow down or kill even the best designed integration effort. As a result, you need to anticipate potential resistance and develop a plan to counter each component of it.

Apart from defending the past, other factors that give rise to resistance include

- fear of the unknown (changing work rules, duties, processes, and procedures)
- fear of failure (an inability to learn or perform under newly integrated processes or procedures)
- a loss of power or control (the taking away of status, resources, promotional opportunities, and job security).

You must plan for resistance, but you should expect support from leaders of already closely integrated functions such as the supply chain, finance, marketing, and brand management; managers and employees with a background in process reengineering; Six Sigma specialists, fast advancing high potentials unmotivated by the status quo; and candidates and new hires.

Measuring Your Success

No effort should proceed without one final planning step: a list of metrics or measures and current baseline data that can be used for determining whether the integration effort between any two activities improved performance. Typical metrics to consider include improvement in process time, process error rates, process costs, user satisfaction, user complaint rates, and the average perceived level of cooperation as rated by employees of both activities.

Final Thoughts

For years, organizations such as Walmart, FedEx, and the U.S. military have demonstrated the significant positive impact that results from closely integrating operational processes. Unfortunately, most leading-edge process integration efforts have historically originated in business units outside HR. Though HR might have been able to avoid a high level of integration, all global HR functions are now expected to be fully integrated. The talent acquisition function in particular is also becoming more interdependent, diverse, and complex as a result of its increased use of social media. With this increased complexity and dispersion, closer cooperation and integration become more necessary but also more difficult. Recruiting leaders must immediately begin identifying and breaking down the barriers that slow results and that frustrate stakeholders. Delaying action is no longer an option, and talent management leaders should seize the leadership role as the best integrators within HR.

About the Author

John Sullivan, a professor of management at San Francisco State University, is a provocateur and strategist in the field of human resources and talent management. For more than 30 years, he has offered critiques and insights to professionals seeking to develop a true competitive advantage for their organizations. His work is driven by a relentless dedication to do away with the status quo and drive the development of practices that demonstrate the impact of strategic talent management planning on an organization's financial performance. His body of published work comprises numerous books and more than 700 articles in the *Wall Street Journal*, *Fortune*, *The Economist*, the *New York Times*, *HR Magazine*, *Workforce Management*, and many other newspapers and magazines. When not in the classroom, he travels throughout the world speaking to and working with the heads of leading organizations.

Hiring the Best: The First Step in Integrated Talent Management

Leslie W. Joyce

The journey of a thousand miles begins with a single step.

—Lao Tzu

I've been teaching leaders to recruit and select people for 25 years. Since my first real job in human resources, I've been passionate about the first step in the talent value chain, hiring the *right* people, which makes developing the right skill sets so much easier.

Hiring the right person sets the foundation for every talent activity that follows. Get the foundation wrong—pick the wrong person—and you will be living with it for a long time. As the head of learning and leadership development, I've been in the unenviable position of having responsibility for training all the "right" people that others hired—turning a sow's ear into a silk purse is just as hard as it sounds—and it is terribly expensive.

For an industrial psychologist, "selection," as we call it, may be the hardest discipline to master. It is highly technical, using statistics that are as hard to pronounce as they are to calculate. The impact of error is enormous and can result in spending a lot of money on expert witnesses if you, yourself, do not relish the idea of spending countless hours in a little wooden box at the front of a courtroom explaining the reasons your hiring managers made the decisions they made. Because of this, we psychologists have spent years and years and years designing incredibly complex and completely predictable processes and systems to circumvent the one thing we hate most: the individual opinion and judgment of the hiring manager. Individual opinion is terribly unpredictable, and worse, it's often wrong. Often, in our opinions, if "they" would "just let the system do what it was designed to do," everything would be all right. However, there is this pesky and consistent expectation that leaders should actually get to choose the people who work for them. How selfish is that?

I learned this lesson very early in my career. Despite my great education in the science and practice of employee selection, managers consistently ruined my handiwork by choosing the person they "liked best"—sometimes despite the clear evidence that there were other equally qualified candidates with a far higher likelihood of being successful.

So once I gave in to the reality that personal choice is actually a good thing, I decided that maybe I could help hiring managers make better decisions about whom they chose and why. If I could help them appreciate the magnitude of the decision they were making, and thus really consider the importance of what they were doing, maybe my processes would have more value in the overall decision-making scenario.

Among other things, I came up with a brilliant (my opinion only!) exercise—shown in the sidebar—that I thought did a good job of demonstrating the magnitude of the decisions they were making. I often found this exercise quite helpful in setting the tone at the beginning of a training class or as a spontaneous table exercise when making presentations on talent management to big groups. It can also be reduced to just the most salient questions to make your points. Take a few minutes and try it.

The first few times I did this exercise, I was amazed at how successful it was, and I have used it ever since. It has continued to hold true

My "Brilliant" Exercise

1. Take out a piece of paper and draw a vertical line down the middle. Then make seven horizontal lines to create a two-column grid.
2. Next, think about your most recent new car purchase.
3. Write "CAR" at the top of the left-hand column.
4. Answer the following questions—one at a time—and place the answers sequentially in the boxes below "CAR" in the left column:

   - What is the make and model of the car?
   - How much did you pay for the car (total with taxes)?
   - How much time (in minutes, hours, and/or days) did you spend researching your choices/options before you purchased the car?
   - How many different sources of information did you consult before purchasing the car?
   - How many other cars did you consider before purchasing this car?
   - How many people were involved in helping you make your decision?
   - How long do you plan to keep the car?

5. Now think about your most recent hire.
6. Write "NEW HIRE" at the top of the right column.
7. Answer the following questions—one at a time—and place the answers sequentially in the boxes below "NEW EMPLOYEE" in the right column:

   - What is the role and function of the new hire?
   - What is the annual, fully loaded salary of the person you hired?
   - How much time (in minutes, hours, and/or days) did you spend looking at potential candidates before you chose this person?
   - How many different sources of information did you use to source candidates?
   - How many other candidates did you consider before hiring this person?
   - How many people were involved in helping you make your decision?
   - How long do you want this person to work for you/for the company?

8. Look at the difference between the left and right columns and think about the following questions:

- On which did you spend the most time before making a decision?
- Which cost the most money?
- Which do you want to keep the longest?
- What is the "return on investment" for the car versus the new hire?

9. Ask yourself: Did you spend more time and less money on the decision to purchase your car than your new hire?

10. Optional discussion questions:

- If you get tired of the car, will you sell it, trade it in, or give it away? If you get "tired" of the employee, what will you do?
- Having had the car a while, are you still proud of the decision you made? How about the employee—still proud? Is that car or that employee a good reflection of you?
- Would you recommend the car to your friends if their needs were similar to yours? How about the employee?

even as the prices of cars have increased. Sometimes, this is the only comparison I have had to provide to change a person's behavior. It is easy to see that in the long run, an ill-considered hiring decision costs the company, and the manager, a carload of cash. However, before you get to the point of making the decision of whom to choose, you need a pool from which to choose. The exercise emphasizes both the creation of the pool (candidates and sources) as well as the decision-making process. The quality of your talent pool is both your first hurdle and your first accomplishment. Recruit effectively and you increase your chances for success.

Fish Where the Fish Are—Six Steps in Effective Recruitment

As my mother always said, there are lots of fish in the sea, so be a good fisherman and find the best that the sea has to offer. The question is: Where are the best fish? During the last few years, I've determined that there six key steps in creating and communicating a compelling argument that top talent ("fish") cannot ignore and that will thus enable you to effectively recruit them.

The first step in effective recruitment is to identify the talent acquisition strategy that best supports your business strategy. Your talent strategy is a conscious decision regarding what methods and approaches will most effectively enable you to identify, source, and secure the best talent in the market. Organizations face many choices, but they can be distilled down to four fundamental strategies to get the talent you need to realize your business strategy:

- Will you *buy*—hire externally?
- Will you *build*—develop internally?
- Will you *borrow*—hire for a defined timeframe?
- Will you *bind*—provide incentives to attract key talent to stay?

Each of these four talent strategies works best in certain business conditions, and each has its particular pros and cons. Perhaps the best news is that each strategy complements the others, enabling an employer to use multiple strategies at once, or in succession, as business conditions and business strategies evolve.

The second step in effective recruitment is to create a compelling employment value proposition that clearly states what is different about your organization versus others that top talent might consider. Successful companies have a compelling customer value proposition—a proposition that clearly articulates what makes it a better place to shop at or invest in than its competitors. Increasingly, a successful company also has a compelling employment value proposition that clearly represents the benefits of working for it versus its competitors—a proposition that has three key elements: differentiation, credibility, and sustainability.

The third step in effective recruitment is to capture the employment value proposition in a memorable employment brand that simply states what makes your organization a great choice. In its simplest form, an employment brand is a "tag line" that grabs the job seeker's attention and compels him or her to consider your company. The employment value proposition, the employment brand, and all the supporting recruiting material are the foundation of an employment marketing campaign, whose purpose is to put the employer front and center with the talent it seeks.

The fourth step in effective recruitment is to translate the employment brand into a talent brand that clearly articulates the caliber of talent working for your organization. The "talent brand" is a description that simply and efficiently describes the kinds of people who work for the organization, the kinds of talent the organization seeks, and the kinds of talent that succeed there. This brand is an essential element of attracting, recruiting, and hiring superior talent.

The fifth step in effective recruitment is to determine the most productive channels to the talent you want. The 21st-century job seeker's options are bigger and brighter than ever before. There are more "channels to market"—that is, ways to contact, connect, and interact with potential employees and employers—than ever before. These channels take a variety of forms, ranging from traditional processes (advertising, search firms, and referrals) to more innovative web-based processes (job boards, communities of practice, and social networking sites such as LinkedIn and Facebook) to truly cutting-edge channels such as virtual worlds and multiplayer games (SecondLife, America's Army, and the like). Channels are available to job seekers 24/7, and they allow employers to connect to local talent or global talent. With just the click of a mouse, an organization can become a major force in the war for talent.

The sixth step in effective recruitment is to measure your success. "If you don't measure it, it doesn't matter," "You get what you measure," and other similar common sayings underscore the importance of measurement and metrics. Metrics can be split into two categories: tactical metrics, which tell you how you've done or are doing (for example, time to fill and applicants per position), and strategic metrics, which tell you what is coming and what you should prepare for (for example, workforce demographics, seasonality, and anticipated job growth).

So you've followed these six steps and have them on the hook. Now how do you get the best fish into the boat? By using the best bait, of course. And in this case, the best "bait" consists of well-designed selection tools and processes.

Good Selection Tools Are Critical

If your goal is to hire the best, you must spend time, energy, and money to develop selection tools that differentiate the good from the very good and the very good from the best. Let's go back to the car-buying exercise in the sidebar: If you don't find and apply rigorous standards to the choices you face, you'll end up with a suboptimal automobile that you'll soon be looking to sell or trade. Unfortunately, however, if you choose suboptimal talent, selling or trading them is often not an option.

My advice is: First, always develop and implement well-designed and easy-to-use selection tools that fit the position for which you are hiring. Second, use a combination of tools to get the best result. What do I mean by tools? Here are a few examples:

- Screening tools—which include telephone, online, or in-person questionnaires designed to quickly identify those who do not meet key criteria.

- Interview tools—which include structured interviews, behavioral questions, and situational judgment scenarios to help uncover past successes and suggest future successes.

- Behavioral tools—which include assessment centers, work samples, and job simulations to give great insight into work-related behaviors.

- Job fit tools—which include assessments that focus on the extent to which a person fits with the company and team they would be joining and the position they would be accepting.

These are just a few examples, and of course, there are plenty more where these came from. If you do a lot of hiring, it is in your best interest to ensure that you have an industrial/organizational psychologist available to you to design great selection processes. It will save money in the long run.

As you can see, an effective talent acquisition strategy has many moving parts. All these parts need to work together seamlessly to send a consistent and compelling message to your talent targets. Working together is not limited to integrating the various components of talent management and/or HR. The secret sauce, if you will, is the total integration and alignment of all the talent management efforts within the organization— and this includes employee and candidate touch points both within and outside HR. Each has the potential to impart important information to recruits and candidates.

Alignment Is the Secret Sauce

There are two critical areas of alignment. *The first critical area is the alignment between the organization brand and talent brand.* It's said that if the reputation of an organization's products and services is its face, the talent brand is its heart and soul. If the talent brand and the organization brand are inconsistent, even slightly, then the credibility of both is at risk. To ensure that alignment is created and sustained, it is useful to work closely with the marketing and public relations departments. These include professionals who craft and protect the organization's brand, and they can be an enormous help in creating and protecting the talent brand.

The second critical area is the alignment between the talent brand and the organization's selection and development processes. Alignment starts with ensuring that the parties responsible for staffing, training and development, and talent management are fully aware of the organization's existing or desired talent brand. And alignment depends on partnering with others to ensure that

- Job descriptions and position postings reflect the characteristics of the talent brand.
- The applicant tracking system is optimally configured and functional to ensure that candidate management is proactive and comprehensive.
- Website information reinforces both the organization's brand and the talent brand.
- Onboarding and assimilation processes reflect and make real the promises of opportunity made by the value proposition and the brand.
- Training and development tools and programs are clear and support career development and growth.

Confidence that "what you see is what you get" is critical to building sound relationships with talent prospects. In today's highly connected world, it takes very little time for the failure to deliver on a promise to be shared with others. And once trust is lost, it is very hard to rebuild.

The most talented people expect to get better, and they want the company for which they work to share this responsibility. So once you hire them, make sure you invest in their development and reengage them at every opportunity.

Invest in the Best

I've been doing engagement survey work for a long time, and it seems that three areas always need improvement—compensation, communication, and development. I have yet to find a survey that shows that employees have enough money, know all they want to know about what's going on in the company, and have too many training and learning opportunities. I'm not certain it is possible to pay enough or communicate enough, but I know we can develop talent enough.

We all know that formal talent development processes are the easiest way for employees to see that these development opportunities exist. We also know that informal, experience-based development is the most productive and effective. So it is up to us to provide both formal and informal opportunities. And it is up to us to build organizations that use all the tools available to invest in the great talent they hire. The best way to keep great talent is to enable them to become even better.

Summary

Today's top talent has an unprecedented variety of employment opportunities. And at their fingertips, they have extraordinarily thorough and quick tools for job searches. In this highly competitive and fast-paced climate, a one-size-size-fits-all strategy to attract and recruit talent will not attract the best. Therefore, to be successful, employers need to

- Have a clear talent strategy—whom do they need, and where will this talent come from?

- Know and understand what is important to today's workforce and reflect that in the employment value proposition.

- Be educated consumers about the pros and cons of every talent channel.

- Use terrific tools for selecting the best in the talent pool, and structure your interview processes to focus on skills and organizational fit.

- Invest in developing the talent that you worked so hard to hire.

Talent is the great differentiator—the one thing that cannot be copied quickly by other organizations. The winners in the talent war have sound talent strategies and rich productive talent channels. They ensure that excellence in attracting and recruiting talent continues into their selection and development processes. Having *the right talent in the right place at the right time* is the ultimate goal. Sourcing the right talent is only the beginning of the equation—the first step in the journey.

About the Author

Leslie W. Joyce is chief talent officer at Novelis, Inc., the world's leading provider of rolled aluminum products used to create sustainable containers, building materials, and automobile parts for many of the premiere brands around the globe. Before joining Novelis, she spent almost seven years leading the organizational effectiveness function and serving as the chief learning officer for The Home Depot. Previously, she led the global organization research and development function for GlaxoSmithKline. As an active member of the Society of Industrial and Organizational Psychology, she has numerous publications and presentations to her credit. She is the founder of the Leslie W. Joyce and Paul W. Thayer Fellowship in Industrial Psychology, which provides financial assistance to graduate students interested in an applied career in training and leadership development. She received a PhD in industrial psychology from North Carolina State University.

Section III

Compensation and Rewards

Aligning Learning and Development With Compensation and Rewards

Jon Ingham

Ensuring the alignment and integration of learning and development with compensation and rewards—and other management policies, processes, and practices— is an important aspect of effective talent management. There is, first, a need for horizontal alignment— ensuring that both L&D and C&R, along with other elements of the HR and management architecture, are linked together and support one another.

However, it is even more important for an organization to ensure vertical alignment, which it achieves from having both L&D and C&R, and other processes, aligned with its overall business strategy and its mission, vision, and values.

One helpful concept is organizational capability. This consists of human, organization, and social capital and acts a bit like the organizational equivalent of an employee competency framework.

Organizational capability provides strategic focus in the same way as clear competitive positioning or a set of core competencies, but it is more concerned with what the organization sees as important in its people rather than just its processes and technologies (core competencies) or simply its products, services, and customers (competitive positioning). This is useful because it helps an organization refocus from HR activities to human capital as an outcome of these activities. This focus on human capital and organization capability can then also make it easier to link L&D, C&R, and other HR processes with the business strategy.

These vertical and horizontal linkages can help build HR, L&D, and other processes around what an organization believes about people management and development—for example, what it thinks works in motivating and upskilling people and how these strategies can best be implemented.

Differentiation in L&D and C&R Systems

One source that has had a high impact in the C&R area recently is Dan Pink's book *Drive: The Surprising Truth About What Motivates Us* (2009). Pink suggests that a lot of what we try to do to motivate people (at least those working in knowledge management roles) fails to do its job and can actually produce the opposite result from what has been intended—that is, less motivated employees. Organizations that subscribe to Pink's thinking will look to use other forms of reward and recognition than just pay and, in particular, will work toward creating an environment in which people can motivate themselves. As part of this, these organizations are also more likely to make greater investments in learning and to see doing this as providing a source of motivation and a basis for capability development.

In thinking about what works in strategy implementation, some organizations will decide to focus more on competencies and others more on performance. Focusing on competencies is still a popular approach to developing strategies in L&D and other areas of HR, but is now less common in C&R than it was at the end of the last century. The problem with a high emphasis on competency-based rewards is that organizations can end up paying for characteristics that do not always lead to enhancements in performance. However, this means that today there is a common potential misalignment, whereby organizations focus on competencies for L&D and on performance for C&R. This is not necessarily a problem but could mean that L&D is suboptimized, so the situation does deserve some consideration.

To give another example, some organizations believe strongly in formal systems and structures, whereas others prefer informal and social ways of operating. The first form of organization is likely to have set learning curricula for each grade and level supported by an L&D management system. Organizations subscribing to more informal approaches are likely to put a greater emphasis on opportunities for connecting with others in the organization and for self-managed learning. An organization's C&R strategy should also be aligned with these approaches to learning. For example, a formal L&D system is likely to function best when supported by a formal incentive program, and an informal or social approach to learning may work best when linked to a looser recognition program that allows and encourages managers and employees to express their appreciation for exceptional effort, skills, and performance.

L&D, C&R, and other process areas should also be affected by an organization's staffing model, that is, by the way it recruits, exits, and progresses staff through its career levels and grades. An interesting example is provided by looking at legal, accounting, and other professional services firms. The staffing models in many of these firms are built around the requirement for staff to gain professional qualifications before they can become highly chargeable and therefore more marketable. Referring to his recent book *Talent on Demand: Managing Talent in an Age of Uncertainty* (2008), Peter Cappelli describes these firms as academy organizations and suggests that their staffing model is unsustainable because staff will easily be poached once they have gained their qualifications. In my experience, however, this only becomes a problem when L&D and C&R strategies are out of alignment or when organizations are not sufficiently creative to develop broader methods for retaining their people.

So, for example, when I was an HR director with Ernst & Young, we put significant effort into linking C&R with L&D, and in particular focused on ensuring that employees' compensation was increased substantially once they had received their accountancy qualifications. But we also focused on making the firm a real employer of choice, so staff members knew exactly how they would benefit significantly from working for it as opposed to its competitors. And we ensured that these benefits were provided not only in rewards and learning opportunities but also in many other areas.

These vertical and horizontal linkages can also be useful for thinking about particular issues within talent management. For example, one challenge for many organizations operating in Western countries is the aging workforce. Increasing and often unpredictable retirement eligibility criteria are accelerating the trend for employers to introduce new roles for older workers, enabling them to focus on coaching and supporting the learning of younger workers, and also supporting knowledge transfer before they leave. Though not so prevalent, these challenges are also leading some organizations to rethink their C&R policies, allowing them to retain older workers without necessarily continuing to increase, and maybe even to decrease, rewards. This raises interesting questions about how these organizations will encourage older employees to continue to invest in their own learning while not benefiting from any further increases in rewards. (The answer to this question seems to focus on emphasizing how these individuals can be recognized other than through more pay.)

Choosing L&D and C&R Strategies

The important thing to understand from all this is that there is choice— people management and development strategies can and should look different from one organization to another. What counts isn't best practice; it's best fit.

This differentiation can come in a number of ways, including by building an organization's HR architecture around a particular capability, staff model, and the like. However, one basis for organizational differentiation is the extent and type of employee differentiation. Many organizations are increasingly focused on differentiating their best performing from their lowest performing employees, an approach further popularized recently in *The Differentiated Workforce* (B.E. Becker, M.A. Huselid, and R.W. Beatty, 2009). However, a smaller number of organizations believe that excessive differentiation can result in internal competition and lead to reduced collaboration. Many of these organizations want all their people to perform at similar levels—whether this is due to their management philosophy or is the result of focusing on a particular type of role where standardized performance is important. Where an organization stands on this spectrum will, or at least should, influence the approach that it takes, including to L&D and C&R.

An organization that wants to treat people equally is going to be more likely to offer standardized menus of development activities and to set rewards at team rather than individual levels. It may also try to keep differentials between high- and low-paid employees quite small. An organization that is more concerned with differentiating its employees is more likely to encourage people to seek ways of meeting individual development needs and to offer opportunities for significantly higher rewards for higher performance, perhaps through a focus on variable rather than fixed remuneration.

You can get a good feel for the variety of opportunities available by comparing organizations at opposite ends of this spectrum. For example, Whole Foods limits its chief executive's salary to $19 for every $1 that the average, full-time team member earns, and the top five executives receive less than 10 percent—as opposed to an average of 75 percent—of stock options. In comparison, Netflix avoids internal benchmarking, instead aiming to pay each employee what they would be able to get elsewhere.

The Benefits of Integration

Integrating L&D, C&R, and other people management processes provides a number of benefits. The first is helping to avoid the common problem whereby an organization is trying to develop one thing but is rewarding another—for example, emphasizing training in technical skills but paying employees more to take managerial roles. More important, it is only by achieving tight integration that organizations can gain the full benefits from all their talent management practices.

When organizations have this level of integration, they can start looking for new opportunities for both L&D and C&R—for example, when learning becomes reward (by promoting the outcomes of learning, holding ceremonies, presenting certificates, and so on) and reward starts to form the basis for learning. Another example of this approach is in gaming, which is increasingly being introduced and adapted into organizations and in which being provided with instant feedback produces immediate, or at least short-term, performance improvement.

Think of an organization with a particular focus (that is, core competency or organizational capability) in innovation. For this focus to be successful, both L&D and C&R need to support ideation, idea selection, and other activities. However, both L&D and C&R might start to have more of an impact if they were combined. This might involve a system of peer recognition providing funding for the best new ideas and an opportunity to develop these ideas (providing learning as well).

Taking Action

What should talent management strategists and L&D, C&R, and other practitioners do to achieve these benefits? The first thing is simply to think about what the opportunities for horizontal and vertical integration might be within a particular organization, given its strategy, environmental context, and so on. In doing this, practitioners should keep in mind that integration can be achieved through either outcomes or activities.

For example, an organization focused on collaboration and treating its people equally (as referred to above) may want to implement strategies for developing the social relationships among these people. It can achieve integration in doing this by using similar activities such as social learning (social-networking-media-enabled learning) and social rewards (for example, social recognition systems providing the opportunity to share kudos with other employees). Both of these involve the use of social networking media to integrate activities across L&D and C&R. Or the organization can achieve integration by focusing on similar outcomes, for example, using learning to develop shared mental models (as in "the learning organization") and lower differentials plus pay transparency to enable smoother collaboration across organizational levels. Both of these involve a focus on similar outcomes but not necessarily similar types of activity.

However, many organizations are going to want to differentiate their employees, and here it is important to consider which people the organization is going to focus on for differentiated support; that is, who are the organization's talent groups, and are they the same or different for C&R and L&D processes? (There may be good reasons why these groups will be different—for example, when different groups are affected by requirements for greater capability and motivation or retention. But practitioners should still think through the consequences of these groups being different.)

Practitioners should also note that integration between L&D and C&R will be supported by broader integration with other processes, particularly recruitment and performance management. Technology integration is also important—allowing information on participation in and success in learning to be linked to reward systems, providing the ability to reward learning.

The integration of metrics also supports integration between L&D and C&R. This integration can also happen at both activity and outcome levels. For activities, the organization can use common metric frameworks for both L&D and C&R processes. For example, many learning practitioners use Kirkpatrick's model, often with the addition of return-on-investment as the basis for evaluating their learning provision. But this model is actually just one example of a standard value chain involving input, activity, output, and business impact / return-on-investment, which can also be used to measure and evaluate C&R and HR processes. Using a similar model across processes helps monitor the success of talent management activities and is particularly useful in evaluating integrated approaches. Organizations can also think about using metrics that will integrate the measurement of outputs, which might include, for example, the proportion of learning that is accessed by people receiving top-quartile compensation.

In general, there will be no need to implement all these forms of integration. But practitioners and other executives should be aware that in most cases, the more L&D and C&R processes are integrated, the more successful talent management strategies are likely to be.

References

Becker, B.E., M.A. Huselid, and R.W. Beatty. 2009. *The Differentiated Workforce*. Boston: Harvard Business Press.

Cappelli, Peter. 2008. *Talent on Demand: Managing Talent in an Age of Uncertainty*. Boston: Harvard Business Press.

Pink, Dan. 2009. *Drive: The Surprising Truth About What Motivates Us*. New York: Riverhead.

About the Author

Jon Ingham is a consultant, researcher, writer, and speaker focusing on strategic human capital management, HR 2.0, and management 2.0. He helps organizations gain competitive advantage through the creation of human and social capital supported by effective leadership, HR and management practices, organizational development solutions, and the use of Web 2.0, social networking media, and the like. He has worked for 20 years in engineering, IT, change management, and HR (including serving as an HR director). He is based in Britain but has a global focus and spends much time in North America as well as Europe, the Middle East, and Asia.

Integrating Learning and Development With Compensation and Rewards at Hertz: A Case Study

Karl-Heinz Oehler

To state the obvious, the world has changed. But more important, the world of human resources has changed. The question is, how obvious are the consequences of this change to the HR community and, more to the point of this chapter, to the learning and development profession?

The L&D profession needs to evolve to keep up with the pressing challenges that organizations face in today's rapidly changing and turbulent business environments. In these contexts, organizations' effective transformations hinge on an L&D model of adaptability and resilience whereby L&D is systemically positioned to manage for results and returns on investment.

As HR professionals, we understand that development programs alone do not foster sustainability, which requires enablers that direct employees' energy and motivation toward adopting newly acquired knowledge and advancing skill development through on-the-job application. Unless the employees who receive the transfer of knowledge in the workplace are properly compensated and rewarded, the developmental impact will evaporate rapidly. That's why integrating L&D with compensation and rewards (C&R) is a powerful tool for delivering real-time, business-focused, development solutions reinforced by incentives to continue desired behaviors for sustainability.

So how did Hertz, the largest general use car rental brand in the world, leverage the synergies of L&D and C&R to make an immediate impact on its business goals? Here, I share the five key success factors we learned along our journey to transforming the L&D organization to focus on results.

Lesson 1: Integrate Systemically, Not Partially

Lesson 1 is to integrate systemically, not partially. At Hertz, L&D continues to be a challenging yet exciting endeavor:

- Challenging—because the ongoing turbulent economic environment requires increased learning agility from employees and creative, yet cost-effective, business-focused L&D solutions.

- Exciting—because socioeconomic changes drive the need for L&D to transform and reinvent itself as a business enabler.

This volatile business context has accelerated the need for Hertz to implement integrated structures, thus eliminating silos not only within HR but also across the entire enterprise. An independent training structure, overlapping curricula, staff duplication, and ineffective delivery mechanisms created our initial learning landscape. Before we integrated L&D and C&R, we first focused on consolidating existing, independent training structures into one global Hertz L&D organization. This integration had clear objectives:

- Drive real-time L&D for real-time results.
- Ensure the transfer and application of knowledge to create sustainable effects on the business.
- Bridge the gap from individual learning to organizational learning.
- Deliver business-focused learning solutions, not training programs.
- Link C&R to changes driven through L&D.

Specific tasks—such as instructional design, program delivery, training administration, and training platforms—were outsourced to a global L&D provider. The new L&D structure consisted of subject matter experts working as learning business partners dedicated to senior business unit leaders and senior functional leaders. The learning business partners were intimately linked with and integrated into the business. They understood both the day-to-day operational problems and the longer-term strategic issues, and they worked in partnership with the business leaders to build solutions. Their intimate business knowledge enabled the learning business partners to develop integrated L&D solutions and define how to measure behavioral changes in the workplace and to compensate and reward the employees being persuaded to adopt them.

Finally, a *global* talent management organization was created, made up of L&D, talent acquisition, performance and career management, succession and high-potential management, operational excellence (Lean Sigma), and human capital management. Additional functions included organization development and culture and change. Creating this level of integration under one umbrella secured a consistent approach with all the touch points of the employee life cycle, which in turn were all directly linked to C&R.

This new integrated structure operated as a center of expertise with the charter to continuously improve internal effectiveness and thus achieve stronger external competitiveness. Its degree of integration connected L&D to all other talent development functions, with the added value of increased cooperation with C&R.

Lesson 2: Take a Systemic Look at L&D and Its Interdependence With C&R

Lesson 2 is to take a systemic look at L&D and its interdependence with C&R. Our central L&D question had become, how do we build an employee development infrastructure that is (1) not only an integral part of talent management but (2) also fully integrated within HR and, more important, linked with C&R? The challenge became a matter of balance: How do we develop the right employee behaviors for creating positive customer experiences while reinforcing and sustaining desired behaviors through adequate C&R programs? It is L&D plus C&R that equals sustainable employee development for greater organizational performance—and we were up for the challenge.

C&R is interrelated with almost every functional HR domain, but its relationship with L&D is special, yet underestimated. It is special because L&D's role is to enhance employee competence, to bring about behavioral change, and to develop employees' ability to work more effectively. Yet development programs all too often fall short in producing the desired change—and not because these programs are poorly designed or delivered. In fact, many of them receive very high ratings. So what *was* the problem?

Reviewing development programs at Hertz, especially those aimed at improving business results, highlighted the fact that employees were convinced that what they learned was right for the business. However, the C&R system was contrary to the principles learned and thus drove a different behavior. New behaviors can only be encouraged, implemented, and sustained if the employees practicing them are properly compensated and rewarded. This was one of the formidable challenges that Hertz L&D faced.

Another challenge was to identify which behaviors positively affect business results and which C&R systems are relevant for each Hertz business. Or, in other words: Where, by whom, and how is value created, and how is the impact of value creation on business results measured and rewarded? The answers to these questions were found by developing partnerships with the business and by integrating HR—not only L&D and C&R—into the Hertz strategic design process.

Lesson 3: Create Business Involvement and Ownership

Lesson 3 is to create business involvement and ownership. Leveraging L&D with C&R by crossing silo boundaries can only be effective if all other HR functions are integrated. That's not usually the case. To have an impact on business results, HR must be integrated with the firm's overall strategy and hence be part of its value chain. Because CEOs and other key stakeholders focus on business results, only integrated HR programs that affect results represent a legitimate basis for investment decisions. Therefore, it is only by becoming an integral part of this value chain that HR will become an area of major focus for CEOs and other key stakeholders, thus representing a critical factor in their investment decisions and in the firm's measurement of business results.

Before working on L&D's integration with other HR functions—and more specifically C&R—Hertz's executive-level managers needed to take ownership of employee development, compensation, and rewards. Demonstrating, in financial terms, L&D's and C&R's combined value creation in the context of an integrated HR organization secured the CEO's sponsorship, resulting in HR's integration into the Hertz strategic design process.

This integration was a critical enabler for all subsequent decisions aimed at removing functional and organizational silos. HR and its functional domains were now intrinsically linked to Hertz's strategic priorities: customer satisfaction, employee satisfaction, and asset management. This link guaranteed that business investment decisions drove subsequent L&D and C&R investment decisions. Consequently, L&D funding was decided upon early in the investment cycle, with *all* critical interdependencies in mind, thereby demonstrating the need to connect L&D solutions with C&R and the related benefits. Most important, combined L&D and C&R investments were directly linked to business results and were expected to generate a return.

L&D, C&R, and all other HR domains were positioned as a service organization—that is, considered as, and treated like, a business with clearly defined service levels. The intended consequence was that investment trade-offs or cost-saving initiatives would have an impact on combined L&D and C&R solutions, requiring the business to decide which solutions would be eliminated or delayed. As development solutions were directly linked to strategic drivers, any investment reductions invariably affected desired business outcomes. This complex configuration got the CEO's and executive team's attention; figures 7-1 and 7-2 show this integration. (How to sustain the continued involvement of the senior management team is further discussed below as part of lesson 5.)

Figure 7-1. HR's Integration into the Hertz Strategic Design Process

Source: Hertz Corporation.

Lesson 4: Define Key Results Areas, Cascade Objectives for Alignment, and Focus on Execution

Lesson 4 is to define key results areas, cascade objectives for alignment, and focus on execution. Let's use a sales example, up-selling, to illustrate this lesson. Up-selling is a common practice in the service industry. Yet up-selling is also an art requiring salespeople to meet customer expectations while selling ancillary products and services to that customer at the same time. Much money is spent in developing frontline employee competence to sell ancillary services to a client who simply wants to complete a rental transaction. The employee is managing a fine balancing act: up-selling at the risk of negatively affecting customer satisfaction with respect to the rental process or forgoing up-selling and losing incremental revenues but meeting customer satisfaction scores.

Development alone will not resolve this conflict or enable the frontline employee to produce the desired outcome—which, incidentally, appears to include two conflicting objectives: achieving customer satisfaction while creating incremental revenues. The C&R system must provide the employee with sufficient flexibility to make the right decision without feeling penalized. Unless this is achieved, developing frontline employees in up-selling techniques will fail to have a sustainable impact on business results and will be perceived as ineffective and a waste of money and time.

Achieving the desired results is a question of alignment. It is about breaking down corporate goals into manageable units at the business, team, and employee levels. L&D programs address each level and, in partnership with C&R, ensure that reward systems are aligned to motivate employees to adopt the desired behaviors. To maximize alignment, Hertz implemented Hoshin planning techniques to (1) maintain the strategic direction of long-term goals while (2) focusing on executing against annual plans. (Hoshin planning is a process that obtains the desired results only if everybody in the organization fully understands its goals and is involved in the chain of place designed to achieve them.)

Figure 7-2. L&D's Integration Into the Hertz Strategic Design Process

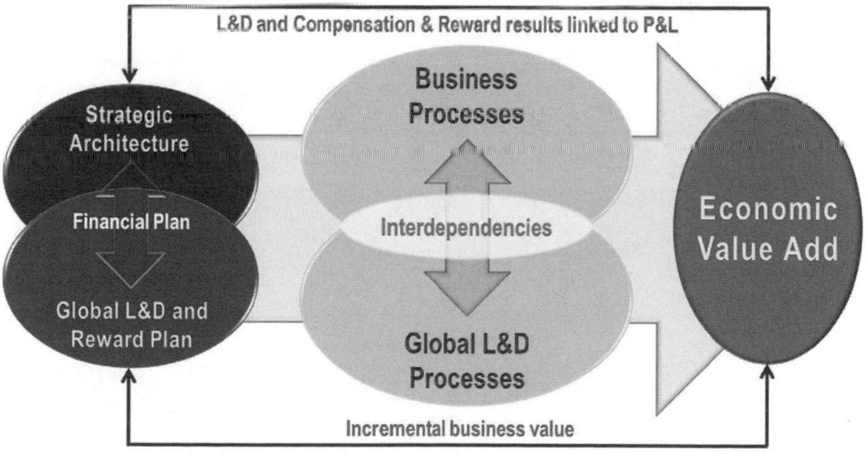

Source: Hertz Corporation.

The starting point is the financial plan to analyze the strategic drivers. Once they are understood, the combined L&D and C&R solution is leveraged to align, develop, coordinate, and adopt a greater focus on desired outcomes. Implemented rigorously, this process makes the concept of "being business focused" real for the senior leaders. It translates planning into execution and thus produces tangible results (figure 7-3).

Last, but by no means least, constant communication between L&D and C&R, and the business leaders for that matter, is of paramount importance to maintain focus on business outcomes. This message cannot be repeated often enough. Business leaders don't like surprises. They value predictability to mitigate risks in a timely fashion. Ongoing dialogue with the business at different levels is a major differentiator to maintain awareness, knowledge, and focus about the status and impact of developmental initiatives on business performance.

Why is this so important? Because markets are volatile and customer reaction to the purchase experience (in Hertz's case, the car rental experience) is immediate. Anticipating changes in customer behaviors enables L&D and C&R to evaluate a specific situation and, as required,

Figure 7-3. Leveraging L&D and C&R to Achieve Desired Outcomes

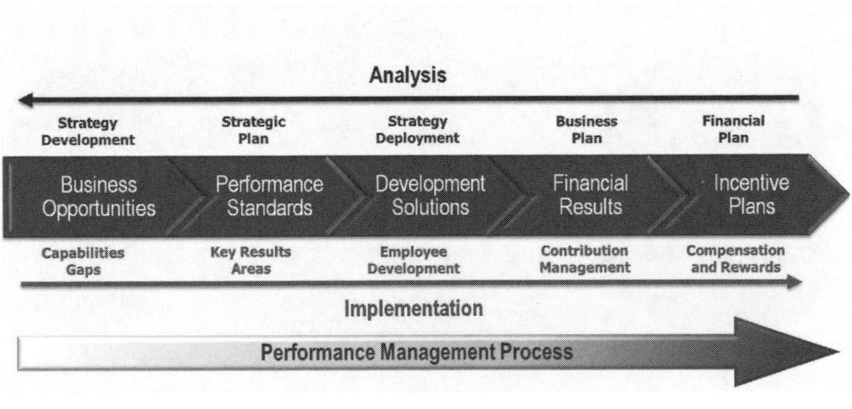

Source: Hertz Corporation.

swiftly adapt their programs to provide real-time responses. This is the art of flawless execution.

Lesson 5: Establish a Business Governance Group to Guide L&D and C&R Decisions

Lesson 5 is to establish a business governance group to guide L&D and C&R decisions. Lesson 3 suggested the involvement of and ownership by the executive team. The biggest risk for managing the integration challenges described above is that senior leaders may disconnect once the programs are under way. Transformation and integration success means constantly working to keep senior leaders engaged. At Hertz, the solution was to establish a cross-functional, senior leadership governance structure.

The L&D governance group meets quarterly and includes the three Hertz business unit leaders and four functional leaders. The role of the group is to review key projects, remove barriers, work collaboratively, set priorities, and drive decision making to ensure alignment with the firm's strategic direction.

The members of the L&D governance group are the highest-ranked Hertz executives, and their active participation and involvement send strong signals to the rest of the organization. They have become role models for change and transformation. During its initial three years, this group gradually started to own the L&D initiatives, and thus it started to set a global direction for the rest of the organization. As the group approved funding decisions based on financial plans, its discussions of development solution budgets became less and less controversial. After all, the budgets that were presented reflected the requirements set under L&D governance, so cutting a budget would mean not doing what the business leaders had asked for in the first place.

This was a fundamental shift away from past budgeting processes. The dialogue with the senior leaders has changed to "OK, I take $X million out of the budget. What is it you don't want me to do?"

Being in this position is a clear sign that our L&D, C&R, and all other HR domains have legitimated themselves in delivering value to the Hertz organization.

Conclusion

Collaboration between L&D and C&R is invaluable for delivering sustainable solutions for employee development. Furthermore, because of the critical interdependencies that L&D and C&R have with the other HR domains, only a fully integrated HR organization will be able to create economic value in the long term. In this endeavor, two questions must remain on everybody's mind all the time:

- What is the most effective L&D strategy to make an impact on business results?
- What is the most effective C&R structure to sustain L&D's impact?

The answers to both questions are intrinsically linked and will vary, depending on the situation. These questions sound simple, but there is a real risk of taking a shortcut to get quick results. However, such shortcuts will most likely prove to be the less effective option because they will ignore cause-and-effect relationships. The result will be a suboptimal solution that will have a negative impact on credibility.

The role of an organization's leaders is to develop, compensate, and reward employees. The role of HR, in partnership with the business, is to provide clear direction for how talent can be best managed and how to leverage the synergy of L&D with C&R to improve organizational performance and value creation. This should never be forgotten—at any point along the journey.

About the Author

Karl-Heinz Oehler is vice president, global talent management, at the Hertz Corporation. His responsibilities include talent acquisition, succession and high-potential management, performance and career management, organizational learning, organization development and design, human capital measurement, and HR due diligence and postmerger integration. A German national, he holds master's degrees in social psychology and economics. He is based in Zurich, having previously lived and worked in South Korea, Singapore, the United States, Finland, Sweden, France, and Germany.

Section IV

■ ■ ■

Performance Management

Creating an Effective Appraisal System

Edward E. Lawler III

The existence of an effective performance management system is often the major differentiator between organizations that produce adequate results and those that excel. Without a focus on performance management at all levels of an organization, it is hard to see how an organization can find a talent-based competitive advantage.

It is far from easy to get performance management right in an organization. The corporate world is littered with companies whose employees never receive an effective performance appraisal. People at all organizational levels go through the motions of formulaic performance appraisals with astonishing insincerity and have little to show for it. There also are numerous examples of situations where individuals thought they were doing the right thing and performing well only to find out they were mistaken when they had their annual appraisals. Finally, in many organizations, performance appraisals simply aren't done, either because of employee resistance or because managers "dry lab" (fake) them.

This chapter is based on *Management Reset: Organizing for Sustainable Effectiveness*, by Edward E. Lawler III and Christopher G. Worley (San Francisco: Jossey-Bass, 2011). Copyright 2011 by John Wiley & Sons. Reprinted with the permission of John Wiley & Sons.

Chapter 8

Performance Management Objectives

An effective performance management system needs to accomplish four things (Lawler, 2008). First, it needs to define and produce agreement on what performance is needed. The bedrock of any performance management system should be agreement on what needs to be done and how it should be done. Without a clear definition of what kind of performance is desired, it is impossible to develop and motivate individuals who can meet or exceed performance standards. It also is key to guiding the performance of individuals so that it supports the organization's strategy and plans.

Second, it needs to guide the development of individuals so that they have the skills and knowledge needed to perform effectively. It also needs to motivate employees to gain the skills and knowledge they need to perform effectively.

Third, it needs to motivate individuals to perform effectively. Even the best talent will perform at a high level only if motivated to do so. When it comes to performance, high levels of both talent and motivation are needed.

Finally, it needs to provide data to the organization's human capital information system. It needs to be the primary source of information about how individuals are performing and what skills and knowledge exist in the workforce. This information is a critical input to talent management as well as to strategic planning.

The research evidence shows that the performance appraisals that are done as part of a performance management system are usually poorly done and, in most organizations, are dreaded both by the individuals doing them and the individuals being appraised. As a result, the failure rate of performance management systems is high. It is tempting to say that the appraisal part of the performance management process wastes more time than it is worth. Indeed, an increasing number of books and articles argue that there is no use even trying to do appraisals right because the appraisal piece of performance reviews simply cannot be done well (Culbert, 2010). It is a kind of "unnatural act"!

The argument against doing performance appraisals usually includes the point that regular feedback is much more effective than is a once-a-year appraisal. If ongoing feedback is provided—and this is a big if—there is no doubt that it is a very important part of a performance management system and can partially substitute for a formal performance appraisal. But it does not provide valid data about the performance of individuals that can be used to determine rewards and support talent management decisions; only an appraisal can provide that.

The message of inevitable failure undoubtedly gives some comfort to those who have failed performance appraisal systems, but it doesn't seem to be leading many organizations to not do appraisals. Indeed, my data show that the recession led to most companies putting more focus on doing appraisals. I think this is the right response; organizations need to do appraisals the right way, not abandon them. So let's look at 10 key principles that need to be built into a performance management system for it to produce high-quality appraisals.

Principle 1: Start at the Top

Principle 1 is to start at the top. The performance management system must start with, be led by, and be committed to by senior management and the board. The board needs to appraise itself and appraise the CEO. The CEO needs to appraise those who report directly to him or her, and the appraisal process must cascade down the organization so that every level experiences it.

In the best of all possible worlds, goals are first set at the top and then cascaded down so that individuals at each level have goals that are tied to the overall strategic direction of the organization. This ensures that there will be alignment in terms of what is done at different levels in the organization and that the strategic direction of the organization will be implemented.

It is not an overstatement to say that if the senior management of an organization is not fully committed to the performance management process, it is simply better not to have a performance management system at all (Lawler, 2003). In this case, "committed" means that executives do not just give lip service to having an effective process. They are willing to be part of the performance management system themselves and to be role models to the individuals who report to them. This is why the appraisal system needs to begin at the board level and cascade down the organization. All too often in traditional organizations, performance appraisal is something "the top tells the middle to do to the bottom."

Principle 2: HR Should Support, Not Own, the System

Principle 2 is that HR should support, not own, the system. In all too many organizations, the human resource function is the owner of, and the implementer of, the performance management system. For a number of reasons, this is the wrong way to position and manage the system. There is nothing wrong with the HR function handling the logistics, but it should not own the system. HR managers should not act as the conscience of the organization or drive and sell performance management. These should be the responsibilities of the top managers.

Principle 3: Cascade Strategy and Goals to All Levels

Principle 3 is to cascade strategy and goals to all levels. The starting point for an effective performance management process should be the business strategy of the organization. It should guide a goal-setting process that leads to individuals, teams, and business units having transparent goals and objectives that are directly tied to the strategy of the business. For this to be effective, the goal-setting process needs to begin at the top of the organization and cascade down. There should be agreement on what will be accomplished, how it will be accomplished, and the measurement processes that will be used to assess whether the goals were accomplished in the correct manner.

Principle 4: Set Measurable Goals

Principle 4 is to set measurable goals. The appraisal system needs to be based on goals whose achievement is measurable (Locke and Latham, 1990). All too often, appraisals are based on personality traits (such as being reliable and trustworthy), vague and immeasurable goals, and a host of poorly defined attributes and outcomes. Measurable goals need to be set, and individuals should be assessed in relation to them. This applies to both the skills and competencies that individuals need to develop and also, of course, their performance deliverables—the how and the outcomes of their performance.

A word of caution is in order here about the mistakes that organizations often make in using goal-driven performance management systems. The most serious mistake involves goal difficulty. The effectiveness of goals as motivators is very much influenced by their difficulty, particularly how difficult they are seen to be by the individuals who have the goals. Easy-to-achieve goals are poor motivators because there is a tendency for individuals to work at a level that will lead them to reach the goal, not at their maximum performance level. Yet very difficult goals—or, as they are sometimes called, extreme stretch goals—are much more dysfunctional.

When individuals feel that they cannot reach a very difficult goal, there are essentially two things they can do, neither of which is a positive. They can simply give up and decide it is not worth trying because the goal and the reward that is attached to it are not reachable. Or they can try to figure out how to "beat the system" to reach the goal. This can lead to unethical behavior, illegal behavior, and excessive risk taking. So goals should be realistic—neither too easy nor too hard.

Principle 5: Set Talent Development Objectives

Principle 5 is to set talent development objectives. The performance management process should not just establish what performance goals are to be accomplished; it should also deal with the skills and competencies that individuals and teams need to accomplish them. It should assess their development needs, plan for their development, and support their acquiring the needed skills.

Individuals should be assessed vis-à-vis their skills and competencies. This is critical, because their skills and competencies determine their value in the marketplace and therefore their compensation level. It also is a key input to the talent management system. Finally, information about them should be a critical input to the organization's strategic planning because it indicates the competencies and capabilities that the organization has and can develop.

Principle 6: Rate Outcomes and Performance, but Don't Rank People

Principle 6 is to rate outcomes and performance, but not to rank people. Setting performance and development goals is the first critical step in establishing an effective performance appraisal process, but it is only the beginning. An effective assessment and scoring of how well the goals are accomplished is the next step. The assessment process should be relatively easy if there are good goals, good agreement on how goal accomplishment will be measured, and the right measurement approach.

Some organizations (for example, ExxonMobil) rank-order hundreds, or in some cases thousands, of people from first to last, numbering them from one to whatever the total number of individuals is in the part of the organization that is being appraised. This effort is like trying to measure the length of an object to the closest thousandth of an inch using an ordinary straight ruler; the information needed to measure performance so precisely just isn't available. Not only does ranking create bad data, it sends the wrong message about how the organization values its talent. Instead of showing a concern for individuals and fairness in assessing them, it sends the message that the organization values structure and rules.

Another seriously flawed rating practice is forced distributions (Lawler, 2002). Some organizations (for example, GE, EDS, and Accenture) require their managers to identify a certain proportion of their reports who are failing, often 5 to 10 percent, and a certain proportion who are doing particularly well, often 15 to 20 percent.

The forced-distribution approach ignores the reality that some work groups have no poor performers and others have no good performers. It causes managers to disown the appraisal outcome and say things like "I was just following the rules; I had to give someone a low rating" when they deal with a "poorly" performing employee.

Forced distributions are particularly dysfunctional when there are automatic reward system consequences attached to individuals falling in different areas of the distribution. A clear example is a program that states that the bottom 10 percent or so of the distribution will be fired each year. Numerous studies show that this produces a great deal of "gaming" behavior on the part of the individuals making the ratings (Lawler, 2008). They do everything they can to be sure they are not faced with having to fire individuals who simply should not be fired. For example, they sometimes transfer them to other functional areas to protect them. Another even more dysfunctional thing some do is to hire individuals whom they think will be poor performers so they will have them available to fire when it comes time for forced-distribution appraisals to be done.

Principle 7: Train Managers and Employees

Principle 7 is to train managers and employees. It is critical that organizations train everyone on how their performance management system works. But it is surprising how many organizations do not do this, given the importance of the system and the fact that it is a relatively complex process that involves behaviors (goal setting and feedback) at which many people are not skilled. The training needed is not just a matter of explaining how the system works and understanding its purpose. Individuals need to develop the interpersonal and feedback skills that lead to effective review sessions. All too often, organizations fail to provide any training to the managers who are expected to execute a performance management system. This is true despite the fact that one of the hardest things for many individuals to do is to give negative feedback to others and to handle difficult interpersonal interactions in a constructive way.

While we are on the topic of training appraisers, it is important to point out that training is also needed for the individuals being appraised. Getting feedback about their performance and reviewing their development is not a comfortable situation for most people and not something that they have the skills to handle well. Thus, the most effective performance management training systems train both the appraiser and the appraisee. A good way to do this is to have the appraiser and the appraisee role-play an actual feedback situation before they go "live" with the appraisal. This is clearly an area where individual coaching can help and is often needed.

Principle 8: Link Rewards to Performance, but Discuss Development Separately

Principle 8 is to link rewards to performance, but to discuss development separately. An important feature of an effective performance management system is the degree to which it affects the reward system; in other words, the degree to which it leads to pay increases, bonuses, stock options, and promotions. Over the years, articles and books have claimed that performance management processes should separate the appraisal of performance from discussions about salary increases and promotions (for example, Meyer, Kay, and French, 1965; Kohn, 1993). This may indeed make some of the discussions easier, but it is not the way to make money and other tangible rewards effective motivators (Lawler, 2000).

Given the importance of goals and money as motivators, it is definitely not appropriate to have a review process that separates the discussion of performance accomplishment and financial rewards (Latham, 2006). They need to be discussed together and tied together so that individuals see a clear connection between how well they perform and how well they are rewarded. Yes, it's true that some individuals work simply for the feeling of accomplishing a goal and, of course, for the mission of the organization. But for others, the relationship between pay and performance is critical to their motivation. The research on this clearly shows that motivation is only likely to exist when there is a direct and immediate tie between the results of a performance appraisal and rewards (Lawler, 2000).

What should be separated from the discussion of financial rewards are the development needs of individuals. Research shows that it doesn't work to discuss training and development at the same time as past performance and rewards (Lawler, 2000). In such a discussion, performance and rewards typically dominate the meeting and prevent meaningful discussions about development activities. Development activities need to be paired with the discussion of future goals and goal accomplishment, not with a backward look at past performance. The key here is combining two future events—performance objectives and what it will take to reach those objectives—rather than combining retrospective events with future events.

Principle 9: Appraise the Appraisers

Principle 9 is to appraise the appraisers. Given the importance of performance management, appraising how well managers perform this task is a logical and important part of the entire performance management process. A good manager simply needs to do good appraisals. Goals need to be set, progress needs to be checked, feedback needs to be given, competencies need to be developed, and, of course, performance needs to be assessed well and rewards need to be distributed. To motivate managers to do these activities well, it is important that they be appraised and rewarded according to how well they do them. The failure to appraise and reward managers for the appraisals they do speaks volumes about the low priority given to this activity.

Principle 10: Consider Having Review Discussions Online

Principle 10 is to consider having review discussions online. The traditional approach to appraisals calls for face-to-face discussions between the appraiser and the appraisee. There are a number of reasons why it is said to be important to have a face-to-face discussion, including the perception that it is likely to lead to better feedback and more meaningful discussions about how performance can improve. That said, there are a number of problems with face-to-face discussions.

Research shows that individuals are very anxious before and during performance reviews (Culbert, 2010; Meyer, Kay, and French 1965). They often don't hear all of what is said to them during appraisals because their mind either shuts down or they are still thinking about something that was said at the beginning of the discussion that they are trying to evaluate and decide how to react to. In short, face-to-face meetings often do not produce good communication between an appraiser and the individual being appraised.

One certain way to improve face-to-face appraisals is to give individuals a draft version of the appraisal before it is discussed, and then have the discussion. This allows the individual to get over what may be the shock that occurs when they first see the appraisal and for them to decide what questions and issues they want to raise. It also allows them to correct any problems in the ratings. It is not uncommon when performance is being measured for bad data to creep in and for an individual being appraised to correctly point out that there has been a mistake. Obviously, it leads to a better discussion if data validity and credibility issues can be resolved before a discussion of the consequences of the appraisal take place.

Organizations should also ask the people who are being appraised to respond and provide input at the end of the performance appraisal period. They should be able to present their version of how well they have performed their work assignments against their preset goals. My research supports the value of giving people this opportunity before their appraiser reaches a performance judgment. It leads to more accurate appraisals and to individuals' believing that they have been fairly appraised (Lawler, 2003).

Let's move to another question: Does there really need to be a face-to-face discussion at all? In today's world, where we interact so comfortably and frequently on the Internet (at least some of us do), it seems quite reasonable and, in fact, potentially more functional to do performance appraisals online. It gives individuals a chance to think a bit before they make their responses and provides an opportunity to check issues for accuracy and meaningfulness. Overall, it may be time to rethink how information technology should be used in performance management systems.

Conclusion

Perhaps the best way to summarize and conclude this discussion of performance management is to say that those who argue for abandoning performance appraisals may well be right when it comes to organizations that are not willing or able to follow the 10 principles presented here. However, by abandoning them, they are giving up on a potentially valuable tool that, when used properly, can make a significant contribution to their organization's effectiveness.

References

Culbert, S.A. 2010. *Get Rid of the Performance Review: How Companies Can Stop Intimidating, Start Managing—and Focus on What Really Matters.* New York: Business Plus.

Kohn, A. 1993. *Punished by Rewards: The Trouble with Gold Stars, Incentive Plans, A's, Praise, and Other Bribes.* Boston: Houghton Mifflin.

Latham, G.P. 2006. *Work Motivation: History, Theory, Research and Practice.* Thousand Oaks, CA: SAGE.

Lawler, E.E. 2000. *Rewarding Excellence: Pay Strategies for the New Economy.* San Francisco: Jossey-Bass.

———. 2002. "The Folly of Forced Ranking." *Strategy + Business* 28: 28–32.

———. 2003. "Reward Practices and Performance Management System Effectiveness." *Organizational Dynamics* 32, no 4: 396–404.

———. 2008. *Talent: Making People Your Competitive Advantage.* San Francisco: Jossey-Bass.

Locke, E.A., and G.P. Latham. 1990. *A Theory of Goal-Setting and Performance.* Englewood Cliffs, NJ: Prentice Hal.

Meyer, H.H., E. Kay, and J.R.P. French. 1965. "Split Roles in Performance Appraisal." *Harvard Business Review* 43: 123–29.

About the Author

Edward E. Lawler III is Distinguished Professor of Business and director of the Center for Effective Organizations at the Marshall School of Business at the University of Southern California. He has consulted with more than 100 organizations on employee involvement, organizational change, and compensation and has been honored as a top contributor to the fields of organizational development, organizational behavior, corporate governance, and human resource management. He is the author of more than 350 articles and 43 books. His articles have appeared in leading academic journals as well as *Fortune, Harvard Business Review*, and leading newspapers. His most recent books are *Talent: Making People Your Competitive Advantage* (Jossey-Bass, 2008); *Achieving Excellence in HR Management: An Assessment of Human Resource Organizations* (with John W. Boudreau; Stanford University Press, 2009); and *Management Reset: Organizing for Sustainable Effectiveness* (with Christopher G. Worley; Jossey-Bass, 2011).

Performance Management That the CEO Cares About

Annmarie Neal and Robert Kovach

In the business world, CEOs have one priority: growth. In the world of talent management, practitioners should have only one priority: their CEO's vision. And so, as one of these practitioners, you should have only one fundamental question: Does your organization's performance management strategy drive your CEO's vision?

The complexity and speed of today's global economy create tension and challenge for today's CEO. Productivity-based performance must be judged relative to today's business models, but at the same time, innovation must be accelerated to create growth for tomorrow. Performance management systems must also seek to optimize performance against these two pivots—managing for today and leading for what's over the horizon.

Three Imperatives

To drive the growth that CEOs need, performance management systems must link to three imperatives:

- business integration
- organizational performance
- an emphasis on return-on-investment.

Business Integration

Validity, reliability, and utility may be attributes of a sound performance management system, but they are not goals themselves. Only a process that is well integrated into business strategy delivers significant value. And to get the true benefits from a performance system, it must become a business imperative, not just an HR process.

Organizational Performance

Today's understanding of success moves the traditional focus from individual performance to organizational performance. Most companies focus on measuring performance on individual units of behavior. But in this new world order, performance is in the collective, and only a successfully managed ecosystem can achieve what we call extreme performance.

Extreme performance can best be described as execution and amplification in multiple business models across the globe, over multiple economic models, while being agile in the face of nonlinear macroeconomic change. Concretely, with extreme performance, leaders can create organizations that will be profitable and grow simultaneously in markets as diverse as India, China, North America, and Europe. To do so effectively, one must fully appreciate the role of collaboration across functions, geographies, and business segments. At Cisco, we accomplish this through our council structure, which requires executives to not only manage their functional remit but also drive cross-organizational strategic value.

Return-on-Investment

Human resources departments naturally gravitate toward an annual process execution of performance reviews. The business naturally gravitates toward return-on-investment. Unless we find a solution that melds both, the CEO will not care because the performance management system will not drive what he or she cares about the most.

The Speed of Business

Even before the "economic inconvenience" that hit global markets late in 2008, the world's business environment was marked by turbulence, complexity, and relentless speed. Never before has the world been so flat, networked, or interdependent. Competition comes from every corner in a real-time, on-demand environment that defies convention and shuns complacency. The capabilities and accessibility of emerging technologies are driving a frenzied pace of change in global economic, political, and market trends. At the same time, knowledge, power, and productive capability are more dispersed than at any other time in history. This complex, decentralized business environment is creating a demand for new operating models, new organizational models, and a new approach to defining and managing performance.

According to the Council on Foreign Relations, the economic models of the 20th century are obsolete and it is time to find new ones. If this is true, then the management models of the 20th century are also obsolete, and those companies that will survive the transition in both cases are those that will be first to win this game.

The Time for Extreme Performance Is Now

Extreme performance is increasingly in demand in today's unpredictable, constantly changing world. Organizations are naturally evolving so that they can thrive in environments where speed, flexibility, creativity, and nonlinear problem solving—as opposed to replication and scaled efficiency, predictability, and linearity—are more and more important for survival and growth. The management theorists and writers of the 20th century such as Frederick Taylor and Chester Barnard focused on how to build efficient organizations. In the 21st century, those theories are at best incomplete as tools to understand what will be effective in the future.

Successful organizations will be able to capture value from traditional markets and, at the same time, capture value from customers with less than a dollar to spend. This leads to a number of key questions, which we can only begin to answer here:

■ How will organizations evolve and be transformed differently? Large multinational organizations will need to execute multiple business models in multiple economic environments simultaneously across the globe. At Cisco, we are developing a dynamic, networked organization that is designed to allow speed, scale, and flexibility when capturing multiple market and technology transitions.

- What strategies focusing on organization alignment, management models, and culture assumptions will induce levels of extreme performance for the business? These strategies will need to include a systemic approach to strategy development, operating model deployment, organizational structure design, and talent management. At Cisco, we adopt a holistic "One Cisco" approach that emphasizes the role of co-creation within the ecosystem—which includes collaboration with customers, partners, and employees.

- How do you encourage an organization to grow by building the talent management systems that drive success, given globalization and its impact on competition, speed to market, and innovation? These talent management systems must solve for creating, capturing, and delivering value across the business ecosystem. At Cisco, the talent management agenda is led by the line executives, with support from the corporate talent management team. We see this as a "team sport," and the line leader is the captain of the team.

- If you're trying to create world disruption, how do you do it in a way that optimizes the past while it simultaneously creates the future? By disruption, of course, we mean something like Clay Christenson's disruptive innovation. At Cisco, we are trying to build the future while having respect for the past. This creates a natural tension between protecting profitable legacy systems, managing performance for today's business environment, and creating the business models of the future. Our leaders have the dual responsibility of both innovating and executing—in essence doing both simultaneously. For example, in our European operations, there is an overlay governance structure that applies focus on running and innovating the business while delivering on quarterly business commitments.

- How do you appreciate the tensions between protecting what has been and creating what needs to be? First, we must recognize that this tension is not only healthy but also necessary when an organization is being transformed. The homeostatic gravitational pull will be toward protecting what has thus far made the business successful. The seasoned, experienced executive will honor this pull while challenging the system to fight against habit and move toward what needs to be.

- With everything going on in the world, how does measuring organization performance change? Performance can no longer be measured by individual achievements and activities. It must evolve toward measuring impact at collective levels—whether this is at the work group, function, or enterprise level. Additionally, it is critical to consider the performance across the entire value chain of the ecosystem. For example, at Cisco, we pay significant attention to partner efficacy and profitability as part of our business practices. In the talent management area, we've adopted this practice to share specific accountability among all the members of the organization and ecosystem who have an impact on the talent agenda.

- What will effective performance look like? Effective performance will look holistic. All parts of the organization are aligned, operating in sync, and able to execute multiple models at various levels in many environments. The difference is akin to playing multiple chessboards simultaneously versus playing checkers. At Cisco, we measure the effectiveness of talent against multiple screens—including functional, segmented, geographical, and that of the organization as a whole.

A Shift, but to What?

In this new world order, performance is in the collective, and the whole is greater than the sum of parts. Consider how quickly Wikipedia disrupted our ideas of how you produce an encyclopedia. In this new environment, we must ask ourselves five key questions:

- How do you measure performance and hold people accountable when output is collective and changing?

- How does this fit with how people have been socialized toward work, the psychology of individual achievement, and the idea that one's success will rely on the success of others? Because the unit shifts from a widget to a complex solution, how do we now measure things that are unmeasurable? This will require looking at the problem from a multidimensional context.

- In this environment, how do we define elite performance and incompetence? How do you assess requirements that will add to the future versus reward historical performance?

- How do we measure performance and allocate rewards across the entire value chain? For example, the macroeconomic ecosystem won't always tolerate technology designed in India, manufactured in China, and sold in Europe just to create profits for shareholders in the United States.

- Should we care about how and whether people are "engaged"? Engagement is a concept more suited to the developed world. Many employees in developing economies are at a lower level of Maslow's hierarchy of basic human needs and seek a job to provide safety and survival. Is engagement a driver of performance management or just an output of a good talent management system?

Even in the absence of definitive answers to these questions, you can focus on several key areas to help you start tackling these questions and aligning your performance management system with your CEO's needs today:

- *Review your competency model and make sure that it aligns with your business strategy.* If a leader performs highly in all these areas, is there a clear connection to how it will affect the business performance? This is not a place to be fuzzy. Be more focused on business strategy and specific effects, not on industrial or organizational psychology. At Cisco, we threw out the business schools and consulting firms and had 200 of our top leaders build our competency model. By virtue of this process, our leadership model is intimately tied to the changing demands of the business. And given the relevancy of this model, executives readily leverage the model in their day-to-day management of leadership expectations.

- *Align rewards with the performance management system.* We know that this is easier said than done. Most systems of rewards recognize past performance at the expense of future potential and value. The ideal system will differentiate and reward for the complexity of the challenge versus the activities one undertakes. At Cisco, our progressive executives look beyond the core performance management tool to create an overlay system that drives goal alignment, robust dialogue, and rewards. While working within the corporate umbrella, these executive-led organizational development interventions drive customization, engagement, and increased performance effectiveness.

- *Develop a system that aligns first to strategy and then has "good enough" validity, reliability, and utility.* We have to overcome our trained tendencies to seek statistical perfection when business alignment is more valuable. At Cisco, our executives expect the performance management system to drive increased productivity, innovation, and business growth. For example, our worldwide head of sales not only completes the requisite tasks within the tool but also leads a parallel process resulting in robust three-way discussions among himself, his leaders, and his talent officer to amplify strategically aligned performance and development messages. These discussions not only result in clarity about actions and deliverables but also allow for a person-centric approach that respects the uniqueness of each leader and his or her career.

- *Ask your executives how they use the system.* Most executives see performance management systems as administrative burdens. Strive to build systems that executives will not only complete but also embrace as part of their leadership platforms. At Cisco, this is an area where we continue to learn and evolve. Though we used focus groups to design our performance system, the organic emergence of overlay practices showed us needs that these groups did not identify.

■ *Give your executives feedback on how they are using the system.* Use scorecards that correlate executive performance assessments with other talent management decisions, such as calibration, promotions, and compensation. The scorecards are presented to each executive so they can receive just-in-time feedback on their executive decision making. At Cisco, we leverage a comprehensive talent scorecard that provides each senior executive with a dashboard that highlights year-over-year trends in ratings of portfolio performance, leadership viability, talent stability, pipeline depth, and the alignment of rewards.

■ *Collaborate.* All too often, performance management systems are built by HR professionals and presented to the business as a finished product. Our internal best practice advocates collaborative design processes that engage leaders early on. Cisco, one of the world's largest technology corporations, deploys a process whereby executive talent management is run by the leaders, for the leaders, through an executive advisory council. This council has governance authority over the execution of the executive talent strategy and architecture delivered to Cisco's Board of Directors. Functions as diverse as strategic positioning, executive development, executive compensation, staffing, learning and development, and the HR partners' organization constitute an ecosystem whose parts come together to work holistically in accord with Cisco's talent agenda.

■ *Challenge the status quo and the HR system.* A traditional approach to performance management measures what has been accomplished retrospectively. What we are saying is that measuring what has happened is less important than creating conditions for business growth at the levels of both the individual leader and the organization. To create a system that your CEO will care about, you must demonstrate the courage to break all the rules and challenge HR performance systems as we've known them. At Cisco, we are managing this tension by acknowledging it and engaging in active discussions about the future role of traditional performance management in a dynamic, networked organization. Given the complexity of the global environment that we have just entered, it is time to reassess the appropriateness of performance models that were created in more stable economic times.

Performance Systems to Accelerate Evolution, Not Just Record History

A performance management system must do more than record history. It must accelerate the performance of the organization. A performance management system needs to focus on and solve for adaptation to creative alignments, various kinds of power expression, and different forms of innovation. It needs to take into account a rapidly changing world where change is dynamic. It must continue to collect and record content. It must mobilize and maximize aligned action. It must consider that disruptive innovation will not come from an individual but from a collaborative ecosystem and nurtured networks.

We end this chapter as we began. In the business world, every business owner and CEO cares about only one thing: growth. If your performance management system doesn't amplify growth, then you are on the wrong side of the tracks. And if culture will eat strategy for lunch, then traditional performance management systems will eat innovation for lunch. Therefore, you must redesign your performance management system at an architectural level and customize it for the growth needs of your business. If you don't, you face the prospect of falling behind or, even worse, getting hit by the train.

About the Authors

Annmarie Neal is the chief talent officer of Cisco Systems. Before joining Cisco, she served as senior vice president of the Global Talent Office at First Data Corporation, where she designed and guided the long-range integrated talent strategy for the company, culminating in a paradigm and culture shift that capitalized on leadership as a competitive advantage. As a senior consultant with RHR International, her work encompassed account management, business development, and direct management consultation with senior executives. She received a doctorate and a master's degree in clinical psychology from the California School of Professional Psychology–Berkeley. She also holds a master's degree in counseling from Santa Clara University, a graduate certificate of special studies in management from Harvard University, and a bachelor's degree in psychology from Boston College.

Robert Kovach is director of the Cisco Center for Collaborative Leadership, where he leads the executive leadership viability efforts for the company. Before joining Cisco, he was managing director of the London office of RHR International; director of human resources for Central and Eastern Europe and Russia with Pepsico, based in Warsaw; and a director of the executive MBA and member of the executive education faculty for both Ashridge Business School in England and the Central European University in Budapest. He has written more than 80 articles and four book chapters on leadership effectiveness and organizational development. He received his PhD in industrial-organizational psychology from Wayne State University.

Section V

■ ■ ■

Succession Management

Managing Succession Successfully for All Concerned

Marshall Goldsmith

Choosing a successor is one of the greatest accomplishments leaders in all key positions can achieve. This chapter mainly examines how to manage succession at the very top of an organization, but the same basic principles apply to the succession process for leaders at all levels. At the beginning of this process, an important issue that will come up is whether to put your energies into an internal or external successor.

Inside or Outside the Organization—Where Will You Find Your Successor?

There are many reasons to choose your successor from *inside* the company, as many companies do (figure 10-1). If you hire an external successor, the board will likely want someone with a proven success record. These leaders are not abundant, and they are not cheap! And if things don't work out, the external hire will likely expect a large exit package. However, the damage from the failure of an external hire is far more than monetary. The negative stories in the business press about such a failure can cost the company severely in terms of its reputation. And the damage exacted by this failure inside the company is even worse, as employees are let go and resources are slashed. Twenty-year company veterans are not happy when they must take less so the failed externally hired leader can leave with more.

When hiring a name-brand leader from outside the company fails, it is often a disaster. Money is wasted, the board is embarrassed, and the perception is perpetuated that high-up leaders are overpaid and executives and board members are self-interested. Seen as part of the selection process, and thus as part of the problem, you and your reputation as the former person in this position are going to go down with the company's.

Finally, external leaders often bring their own entourage of trusted, high-level personnel with them. Internal executives are passed over, promotional opportunities are negated, and leaders at many levels feel they have failed. Valued employees leave the corporation, because they don't

Figure 10-1. Companies Tend to Focus Internally When Seeking Talent

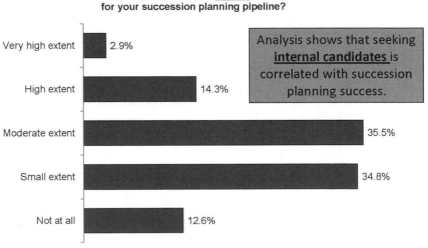

Source: Data collected by the Institute for Corporate Productivity and ASTD.

have high hopes of being promoted in the future and even have fears they may be fired.

This is not to say that companies should not hire externally. There are many companies that do (for example, IBM). However, hiring from the outside does come with high risk. If it is possible to develop an internal successor, that is often the best route.

What Message Are You Sending About Leadership Development?

Hiring from the outside is indicative of a failure in leadership development for the company—at least that's the opinion of one famous CEO with whom I teach in a corporate leadership development program. Ironically, he was hired from outside the company. But he has made it his personal mission to develop talent from within, to develop his own successor.

Leaders at all levels have to answer this question: "If I weren't here tomorrow, who could take my place?" If you can't think of anyone, then you haven't been developing your successor! You have not been participating in what you have been requiring of your line managers. You have not been practicing what you preach. You have not been developing leaders!

Ensuring Continuity of Vision Through Internal Succession

As explained above, hiring a key executive from the outside can bring great risk and send people the wrong message about the organization's leadership development process. The opposite can be said of effective internal succession, which can produce many positive outcomes.

Hiring from the inside shows that you and your organization are developing talent just as you are asking everyone else to do. When you promote from within, it opens up another top-level position, which leaves room for the promotion of another internal executive.

As part of the leadership team, you have a vision for the company, which you want to endure after you leave. Of course, you will want your successor to have his or her own ideas; however, you don't want all your hard work to be negated. Who better to carry on your vision after you depart than someone who has lived it with you over the years?

Business Forces That Eliminate the Chance for Internal Succession

Sometimes forces in the business environment eliminate the possibility of an internal successor, even though this may be your goal. For instance, in one famous case, a high-level executive committed an ethics violation. Though the outgoing leader was not involved in the violation, he was held responsible for the damage. The board felt that it was important to send a message about the severity of the problem and the need for the company to change.

In another case, even though an internal candidate was seen as a potentially excellent leader, the business environment led to the selection of an external candidate who was seen as an even better immediate choice.

How do you decide when not to develop your successor from inside the company? The answer, though complicated at one level, is quite simple at another. Do a cost-benefit analysis. What will it cost to bring in an outsider? What are the potential benefits? What are the costs to promote each candidate? What are the benefits? And finally, are there any outsiders who cannot be matched by someone in the company? If the answer is "yes," by all means hire the outsider. If the answer is uncertain or "no," promote from the inside.

Whether you choose an internal or an external successor, you will probably find that these talents are required:

- The executive will undoubtedly be very bright; stupid people are not often considered for these positions in major corporations.
- You will want a candidate with a history of achieving results.

- You will want someone who is dedicated and committed to the success of the organization and who cares about the company and its people.

- And finally, integrity is an important quality—executives who commit integrity violations should not even be considered for a CEO position, or any other for that matter.

Now that you know what to look for, remember that developing your successor is an extremely personal matter. Your job is to help this person become a great leader for the company, person to person, leader to leader, and that is a great accomplishment! For a detailed example of how this can be done, see the sidebar.

Moving On: Advice to CEOs on How to Exit Gracefully

Succession is a process that every leader faces eventually. Some leaders handle it very well; those who aren't prepared for succession do not. They often regard it as something that will happen "later"—that is, until it is happening, at which point it is too late to prepare.

Rather than be shocked when the time actually does come to leave, how can you prepare for transition? What is the human side of transition? And how can you leave your position with class and dignity?

Preparing for Succession

At some point, you will have to hand off the baton of leadership to the person who will take your place. How you prepare yourself and your successor will determine how successful the handoff will be. You'll have to take two important steps. First, you'll have to slow down, so you and your successor don't drop the baton on the pass. Second, you'll have to coach your successor to speed up and carry the baton.

You'll have to do all this while your team's competitors are running merrily along—so you'll need to keep an eye on short-term quarterly results as well as long-term goals—while an audience of stakeholders watches your every move. Stockholders will be checking to make sure they are getting a return on their investments, analysts will be making sure you are keeping your commitments, customers will be watching to see if you are delivering value, employees will be ensuring that your actions match your words, and your competitors will be watching for any sign of failure or exhaustion on your part.

After a successful handoff, you will quickly disappear from view. There will be no grand hurrah, because if you have done a good job of developing your successor, your organization will be even more successful *after* your departure! The best thing you can hope for is to leave a legacy as a leader who made sure that the values of the organization were carried on even after you were gone.

The Human Side of Succession

The process of readying yourself for succession is often influenced by emotion as much as by logic. You are not a robot; you are likely to experience nonrational hopes and fears and perhaps even a sense of loss as you prepare to move on.

Sometimes leaving your job is like leaving your best friend, as was the case with one of my coaching clients. This gracious CEO shared her personal feelings about leaving her job with me and a group of fellow executives. "It seemed like I was getting promoted every few years. I loved the company, my co-workers, and our customers. Going to work was always a joy for me. . . . The time just flew by—and then one day it was time to leave. It hurt."

As a successful CEO, you are probably very ambitious and hardworking. It is very unlikely that this drive is going to go away when you transition out of your position. Though you may have dreamed of relaxing on the beach, spending more time with your family, playing lots of golf, and going on cruises, chances are that if you really wanted this dream, you would have it already. Make no mistake about it; your family has learned to live without your constant attention over the years. Just because you are now "free" does not mean that they will be falling over themselves to spend time with you. The allure of golf and relaxation will quickly wear off, and you may find yourself bored and restless, longing for the good old days when you were CEO.

The good news is that as you prepare your successor to take over, you should have less to do. My suggestion to you is that you spend this down time planning what you will do with the rest of your life.

Leaving With Class and Dignity

It is easy to fall in love with being a leader. When this happens, it is almost impossible to let go. As a CEO, you've faced enormous pressures, lots of work, and even mind-bending grief and frustration, but let's face it—this job comes with great benefits:

- *Wealth*: You have made lots of money, and though it probably hasn't been the most important thing, it has helped you keep score of how successful you have been. Now, as you make less money, you'll have to use a different measuring stick.

- *Perquisites*: The job of CEO comes with many perks, such as viewing sports events from the company box and having the support of a professional staff. Many retired executives find it hard to adjust doing without these perks. My suggestion is to hire a personal assistant—it will free up your time to do something personally rewarding and decrease your embarrassment when you find you cannot do tasks others have been doing for you for years.
- *Status*: You've been a "big shot" for so many years that it has become part of who you are. People have admired you and sought your advice because of your position. Make peace with the fact that this will change. If you can't, don't retire.
- *Power*: Most CEOs have a higher need for power than other people. This power—defined as "the potential to influence"— has gotten you big results and led to the success of huge projects. When you leave, this power may disappear quite suddenly, and it can be hard to give up.

If you cannot make peace with letting go of wealth, perks, status, and power, you will not have a successful handoff. You will also be letting go of some things on a deeper level:

- *Relationships*: You probably like your staff and co-workers. They may even feel like family.
- *Happiness*: This has also been a great by-product of your position. Of course, you can be happy doing other things, but being CEO has been fulfilling, challenging, and rewarding—all things you love.
- *Meaning*: As CEO, you have had impact on people, products, and the world. This is not a trivial job; it is very significant.
- *Contribution*: If you think about what you are most proud of, it probably has something to do with the contribution you've made to others and to the world. As you get ready to pass the baton of leadership, you will have to find other ways to make a contribution if you are to remain fulfilled.

At the beginning of the succession process, many CEOs are in denial about how much they love their jobs. As they go through the process and add up the personal cost of actually leaving, they lose focus and fail to pass on the baton of leadership with class and dignity. You don't want this to happen to you!

The goal of a successful transition is to get through the process in the most positive way possible. Enjoy your final year or so in office, coach your successor to a position where he or she has a great chance of success, slow down, and ready yourself for the changes ahead as you allow your successor to speed up to take on the challenges of your position.

About the Author

Marshall Goldsmith is a world authority on helping successful leaders achieve positive, lasting change in behavior. He has recently been recognized by The *Times* of London and *Forbes* as one of the world's top 15 business thinkers. He is the author or editor of 31 books, including the *New York Times* bestsellers *Mojo: How to Get It, How to Keep It, How to Get It Back If You Lose It* (with Mark Reiter; Hyperion, 2010) and *What Got You Here Won't Get You There: How Successful People Become Even More Successful* (with Mark Reiter; Hyperion, 2007) and a *Wall Street Journal* number 1 business book and winner of the Harold Longman Award for Business Book of the Year. He is one of a select few executive advisers who have been asked to work with more than 120 major CEOs.

Succession Management at Edwards Lifesciences: A Case Study

Rob Reindl

Edwards Lifesciences is a global leader in the science of heart valves and hemodynamic monitoring, with more than 7,000 employees worldwide. In this chapter, I discuss Edwards' strategies for identifying, developing, and retaining successors and how we measure our success.

At Edwards, the succession plans for critical jobs are proposed following the company's strategic planning process and are confirmed during CEO talent development reviews. Because these critical jobs are closely monitored by the CEO and myself (the global leader of human resources), possible successors are not limited to those in the chain of command under the incumbent. All identifiable talent around the globe is reviewed as possible successors for critical jobs, and a high-potential label is a prerequisite. Our goal is to have a minimum of two successors for each critical job. Successors are identified as ready now, ready in one to three years, or ready in three to five years. If there are no diversity candidates in any of these categories, we ask leaders to list names of diversity candidates and when beyond the five-year mark they might be ready. If a critical job suddenly becomes vacant, the CEO and I would expect a call to discuss possible successors. Then a short list of successors would be profiled and discussed at the next Executive Talent Committee meeting.

Once successors are identified for a critical job, several development opportunities are available to them, as well as to others who have been identified as top talent.

The learning and development department receives a list of top talent names and their respective development needs. The L&D staff works with HR business partners (generalists) to determine training needs for the next fiscal year. It is critical that talent development reviews are held before operation planning so that the manager not only plans for his or her top talent development needs but also budgets appropriately for them.

Another development opportunity determined at this time is an external coach who has been trained in utilizing our 360-degree tool. This tool was customized for Edwards' "Core Competencies"—a set of 10 competencies that we believe represent our values and approach to delivering on our commitments to patients, customers, shareholders, and our own colleagues. At times, we have set up a "triangle"—consisting of the successor's manager, an external coach, and an internal mentor—to develop top talent. Many potential executives who are next in line for a leadership role are assigned a mentor, usually an executive leader in another group.

The most important development that a successor can receive is real-life experience on the job. We believe in the L&D philosophy that 70 percent of learning comes from experience on the job, 20 percent from others' experiences (from mentors, coaches, managers, and so on), and 10 percent from training. At Edwards, we are not afraid to move our top talent around the company or add to their current responsibilities for the right job experience before they are promoted to the next job. A few examples will shed some light on how various jobs or additional responsibilities can really position a person for success.

An Example of a Chief Financial Officer's Successor

Shortly after Edwards Lifesciences was spun off from Baxter Healthcare in 2000, it hired a controller who had several years of financial experience in Europe. After a couple of years of successful performance, the controller was identified as a successor to the chief financial officer, to be ready in three to five years. His development needs to prepare to become CFO at that time included experience with treasury, risk management, tax matters, and working with the outside investor community.

During the next five years, Edwards incrementally added staff responsible for treasury, risk management, and taxes who reported directly to the controller, who thus began to take on these responsibilities on a developmental basis. Additionally, the CEO included the controller on several visits to the investment community. We also made sure that the controller received visibility with the board of directors because of the criticality of the CFO role. No doubt it took some finessing with some of the functional leaders who were told that they no longer reported to the CFO but were now going to report to the controller, but such tough calls need to be made, especially when you are preparing someone for a role like the CFO job. In this case, we also needed to persuade the existing CFO to relinquish these reporting relationships. Fortunately, she had aspired to be a business unit leader, and we felt that she needed some operational experience before taking on that role. So we created a president of global operations role that included global manufacturing, supply chains, information technologies, and quality control. That experience prepared her to become a business unit leader.

Thanks to this process, which essentially involved reconfiguring the responsibilities of both the current and prospective CFOs, we now have a strong CFO, who through development opportunities was set up well for success. So the basic lesson here is that you can ensure a successful succession process by being willing to rethink and revise the job duties of those who are slated for succession and those who may be consequently moving on to other positions. In addition, the person on the road to succession needs to be given the kind of exposure to top management that will ensure a smooth transition.

An Example of a General Manager's Successor

An employee in a midlevel role in corporate development and strategy had career aspirations to become a general manager. At the time, this high-potential employee had no experience in marketing, sales, or managing multiple people and also had no experience with profit and loss statements. We made his next assignment to lead a large, complicated divestiture of one of our global businesses. Following that, he led global marketing for one of our largest business units and then went on to lead all of sales and marketing for the business unit in Japan. His last job before becoming a general manager was vice president of strategy for the entire company. This is a highly visible role with our board, CEO, business unit, and regional leaders. As a general manager, this person now has sales and marketing experience, global experience, and strategic development experience. I imagine that this employee will take on even more responsibilities in the years to come. The lesson to take away here is simple: Give prospective successors a clear path to gaining experience needed for their likely new responsibilities.

Key Lessons

Edwards' experiences yield several overall lessons:

- Know your development jobs.
- Retain top talent.
- Engage your CEO.
- Emphasize results.

Let's look briefly at each.

Know Your Development Jobs

First, it is important to know which jobs are the best development jobs in the company for preparing top talent for large general management roles. These jobs are usually "flow-through" jobs, and the manager of them has to come to that realization. So the managers of these jobs need to have an ongoing talent search for them, because people usually occupy them for two to three years and then move on.

One example of a development job at Edwards is the VP of strategy position, mentioned in the previous example. Three of the five key general managers at Edwards had been VP of strategy before taking on their current position. When serving in this position, it was great experience for them to see the company's entire portfolio and to work each year with all the executive leadership team members on the seven-year strategic plan.

Another example of a development job is a country leader or regional sales and marketing leader role. These roles provide early P&L experiences and real-life experience with strategic planning and having to ensure that sales happen on a daily basis (short-term results). In addition, some of these roles have people who report directly to them functionally (such as finance and HR). Because of these experiences, some of Edwards' best leaders do a phenomenal job at balancing the short- and long-term results.

Retain Top Talent

Make sure all the successors are with your company when it is time to promote them to the next level. You certainly want to reap the reward from the investments you made in them.

There has been a lot of research about the reasons why top talent leaves companies. The usual culprits are their managers, pay, or career opportunities. At Edwards, we proactively provide managers with data that can forewarn them of a top talent's potential departure. A top talent risk analysis is provided to each executive leader annually. Top talent is assessed against data to which most HR departments have access. They include

- pay below 100 percent of that position's estimated market value
- not promoted or given additional responsibility within the last two years
- bonus payout below 100 percent
- more than two managers in the past two years
- manager's employee engagement score below 75 percent
- have not attended at least one training session in the last year

At Edwards, we also strive for differentiation in our compensation programs for top talent. Why do we do this? A few years back, I asked my compensation leader for the average bonus percentage paid to all top talent and the average bonus percentage paid to the rest of the salary-exempt employees. Believe it or not, the percentage for top talent was lower. Why? Because we give them more and we expect more of them. So we decided to treat top talent differently from a bonus target perspective. Our top talent are also treated differently with regard to professional development opportunities, and they may receive additional stock options. Another aspect of retaining top talent is creating a culture in which they can thrive. We've paid a lot of attention to this and thus have created a credo in which we really believe and make very visible. For us, it's all about the patient. We encourage much debate, but in the end our guiding light is *the patient.* Values like trusted partner, bold and decisive, thriving on discovery, and recognizing accomplishments are all things that are very apparent in our culture and that I believe are important for all high-achieving medical device talent to be successful. In short, the important part is to create a culture in which high-potential people can thrive.

Our Credo

At Edwards Lifesciences, we are dedicated to providing innovative solutions for people fighting cardiovascular disease.

Through our actions, we will become trusted partners with customers, colleagues, and patients – creating a community unified in its mission to improve the quality of life around the world. Our results will benefit customers, patients, employees and shareholders.

We will celebrate our successes, thrive on discovery, and continually expand our boundaries. We will act boldly, decisively, and with determination on behalf of people fighting cardiovascular disease.

Helping Patients is Our Life's Work, and *life is now*

Engage Your CEO

Finally, it is important to comment on the CEO's engagement with talent development. I am fortunate to work with a CEO, Mike Mussallem, who has talent development in his heart. He has high expectations for each of those who report directly to him with respect to how they nurture, develop, and engage their top talent. Each year, he sets a performance management objective that focuses on attracting and retaining top talent. This year, his metric for all top talent globally is less than 4 percent turnover. He also expects top performance from anyone in a critical job and at least two potential successors for each position. He views talent management as a vehicle to achieving each of our top priorities. When he is asked what one thing made him successful in his career, his response is that he has surrounded himself with top talent and has encouraged his people to do the same.

Emphasize Results

So what does Edwards Lifesciences look at to determine if its talent management has been successful? We decided that if we believe that it is the

---

What Edwards' Talent Has Produced

- **Initial Performance (April 2000)**
  - Underlying Sales Growth: 1%
  - R&D Investment (% of sales): 6%
  - GP: 44%
  - Stock Price: $14
  - ROE: 4%
  - ROIC: 5%
  - Market Cap: $800 million
- **Current Performance (December 2010)** _{EW LISTED NYSE}
  - Underlying Sales Growth: 13%
  - R&D Investment (% of sales): 14%
  - GP: 72%
  - Stock Price: $80.84 (split adjusted)
  - ROE: 18%
  - ROIC: 16%
  - Market Cap: $9.3 billion   Edwards Lifesciences

---

talent in our organization that determines whether we have successfully executed our strategies and priorities, then why not use the same measurements? Refer to the previous page for the company's results since we spun off from Baxter and became a publicly traded company in April 2000 through December 2010.

Summary

The results for Edwards speak for themselves. During a decade when many organizations faced significant turmoil due to economic conditions that challenged sales growth, Edwards' talent performed extremely well. It is talent that executes business strategies. So why not ensure that a pipeline of talent is being nurtured, developed, challenged, and recognized? I hope this chapter has provided you with ideas that you can implement to ensure that you have a pipeline of talent for the future.

About the Author

Robert C. Reindl is corporate vice president of human resources for Edwards Lifesciences. When he joined the company in 1993, he was responsible for Baxter's Institute for Training and Development and became vice president, human resources, for Baxter's CardioVascular business in 1997. Previously, he was a manager with Arthur Andersen, where he consulted internally on a variety of human resource and organizational development issues and designed management development training. He has also been a communications instructor for Marietta College and Ohio University. He received his bachelor's degree in communication from the University of Wisconsin–Stevens Point and his master's degree from Bowling Green State University.

Section VI

■ ■ ■

Engagement and Retention

12

Engaging and Retaining Talent

Beverly Kaye and Sharon Jordan-Evans

Never before have organizations paid more attention to talent—in the United States and worldwide. Keeping it. Poaching it. Developing it. Engaging it. Talent is no longer just a numbers game; it's about survival. It's about winning market share, investors, new clients, big contracts. Companies depend on their top performers to innovate and provide services that differentiate them from their fierce competitors. They rely on their human assets to thrive. Even in the wake of layoffs or high unemployment, many corporations and industries continue the search for skilled talent to fill key roles at all organizational levels.

Executives, line managers, and the learning and development professionals who support them loudly agree that engaging and retaining talent is a core business initiative. In fact, it has been elevated in many enterprises to the top tier of objectives, on a par with generating revenues and managing costs. It is crucial that learning and development professionals effectively integrate engagement/retention initiatives with other key HR functions and processes. For example, recruiters would ideally have retention goals for all new recruits and would work closely with hiring managers to ensure that talent so carefully selected sticks around for a while. Similarly, performance goals should include retention and engagement objectives, and leadership curriculums should include manager education in the art of engaging and retaining talent.

So we agree that engaging and keeping the best people matters. The question, then, is how to do it. We've studied this question for several decades, researching what employees want most from their work and their workplaces, and what employers are doing to deliver on those wants.

Here is some of what we've learned.

Why They Stay

We've asked more than 17,000 people why they stayed in an organization for "a while" (yes, it's a relative term). Our findings confirm what many others have learned about the most common reasons employees remain at a company (and what will help retain them). The items come up again and again throughout every industry and at every level. The differences between functions, levels, genders, and ages are minor. Here are the top 10 responses, listed in order of frequency of response:

1. exciting work and challenge
2. career growth, learning, and development
3. working with great people
4. fair pay
5. supportive management / good boss
6. being recognized, valued, and respected
7. benefits
8. meaningful work and making a difference
9. pride in the organization, its mission, and its product
10. great work environment and culture.

So there it is—the answer to the mystery of retention. Deliver these things and you'll keep them all! Or will you? These research results can be misunderstood and even misused. Why? Because people differ. Though most of us (98 percent of respondents) will select at least one of the top three stay factors on the list, we will also name a factor not named by our colleagues. One person desperately wants flexibility, another wants fun, and yet another craves stability. But how could we have known?

We can only know, and then deliver, by asking.

Start With a Stay Interview

Start with a stay interview—with every employee you hope to keep. Why are we so willing to conduct exit interviews, but we seldom take the time or summon the courage to conduct stay interviews with the people we can least afford to lose?

Imagine this. Your boss calls you in and says, "I probably haven't told you this often enough, but you are important to this team and to me. I can't imagine losing you. I know we've been through a rough time lately, and I want you to know how much I appreciate all you've done and the way you've done it. I'd like you to know that I want you to hang in here. I'd like to know what you want next. What do you want to learn? What career goals are you thinking about? What can I do to help you reach those goals? I'd like to know what will keep you here. And I'd like to know what could entice you away."

Has a boss ever held that kind of interview with you? When we ask audience members this question, few hands go up. When we ask those few people how it felt, we hear, "Good, great, I felt important and valued." One guy in the audience said, "It felt a little late—it was in the exit interview." Everyone laughed at the irony—we often find out what our treasured talented people really want as they exit our organizations.

Why don't managers (including you) conduct stay interviews? Usually they don't because of *fear*.

Some managers don't hold stay interviews because they fear they won't be able to deliver on employees' requests. This is particularly true during economic downturns and associated belt-tightening. If you think you can't deliver on employees' requests, take these four steps:

1. Tell them (again) how much you value them—for example, "You're worth that to me and more."
2. Tell the truth about the obstacles you face—for example, a pay freeze, project closing down.

3. Show you care about them enough to look into it—for example, "I hear your request. Let me look into it, and let's meet again next Friday to talk about possibilities." (If not now, then when? If not this, then what?)

4. Ask "What else?" Research shows clearly that people want more from work than just a paycheck. When you ask the question "What else?" we guarantee there will be at least one thing your talented employees want that you can give.

Stay interviews are not difficult to conduct, and they yield priceless information. In fact, they might be the most important strategy of the several we describe here. Not only will asking make your talented people feel valued, but their answers will also provide the information you need to customize strategies to keep each of them engaged and on your team.

Some managers need support or encouragement in conducting stay interviews. Train them, have them role-play, and coach them as they try out this valuable approach to learning what their employees want and need.

Which of these matters most to you? Go to www.keepem.com and take the "What Keeps You" survey. You'll see how your answers match all others.

Engagement and Retention in the DNA

One manager told us that his company has successfully woven retention and engagement deeply into the fabric of the organization. This CEO said that he expects it to be in the very DNA of the company. It's not a "flavor of the month" initiative or an event to focus on when time permits. Instead, every manager at every level is expected to spend quality time retaining talent.

Managers need help achieving this "DNA proposition," and here is where they turn to their learning and development professionals for the thought leadership and design of integrated (cross-silo) approaches that achieve both the talent management and business goals. These savvy HR pros link arm-in-arm with managers at all levels in an earnest attempt to engage the hearts and minds of good people from the moment they enter the recruitment cycle until long after they leave the company. It's a cradle-to-grave proposition, including activities during

- *Recruitment:* Not only is it important to find the most talented applicants, but it's equally important to be viewed as the employer of choice with a strong employee value proposition. Think about the unique selling proposition of your organization, and use this information to attract top talent.

- *Orientation:* Also called "onboarding," orientation is step one toward retention of your new talent. It should extend beyond the traditional day-long or week-long timeframe and should involve many members of the new employee's team.

- *Career development and growth:* Our research confirms what many others have found. Talented people want to learn and grow. Some want to be promoted or at least identify career options ahead. Ask what they want to learn this year and then find a mentor, a class, a book, or a coach to help them learn it.

- *Re-recruiting:* Companies must consistently re-recruit their existing talent. Help them match their skills to new opportunities in the organization. Thank them for their efforts and outcomes and spotlight their success. If you're not recruiting your best people, you're the only one who isn't.

If you're interested in building a culture where engagement and retention are in the DNA, you may have some work to do. Here we give 10 concrete steps for getting there. But first, consider: What do you want? What do you have? Where is the gap? How do you close it? As basic as this sounds, this is where you need to start. And make sure that you take the 10 steps given here in a way that's in sync with related processes in other parts of the organization.

Step 1: Appoint a Steering Committee

Step 1 is to appoint a steering committee. Although HRD and other senior leaders sometimes feel they must manage the retention battle by themselves, it's vital to get help from a mixed group of managers and employees who can study turnover issues and work together. Ideally, this steering committee would include professionals from every HR function (for example, recruiting, performance management, rewards, succession planning, learning and development). The interchange among these HR silo representatives will bring breadth and depth to the design of the initiatives.

Publishing a retention steering committee charter in a company newspaper or distributing it to division heads and asking for recommendations might be all you need to do. The committee can turn the charter into a more tailored mission statement. In fact, those two items form an excellent agenda for the first meeting.

Step 2: Analyze Turnover and Exit Interview Data

Step 2 is to analyze turnover and exit interview data. Just remember that exit interview information is valid only if the departing employee trusts the interviewer. Many organizations now use an external firm to conduct those interviews in an attempt to get valid information.

Run some numbers. Assess the cost of losing key talent. Add it up and you might be shocked at the cost of talent lost.

Step 3: Survey Your Leaders

Step 3 is to survey your leaders. To learn organizational beliefs about retention, including role and accountability, ask managers at all levels. Then compare what midlevel managers think to what supervisors or senior leaders think. Who's really in charge of engaging and retaining talent?

Step 4: Conduct a "Future Pull" Session

Step 4 is to conduct a "future pull" session. Leap ahead one year and imagine that your senior team is celebrating an ideal future state of talent retention. Brainstorm and write down the projections. For example:

- "We've retained 95 percent of our top talent."
- "We're known as having a retention culture."
- "Good people are banging on our doors."
- "Customer retention rates have increased 10 percent in one year."
- "We're on the cover of *Forbes* magazine."

Encourage the senior managers to create a long list of descriptors. Then lead the team in an analysis to identify the current organizational realities related to retention. Be sure to include numbers and costs wherever possible—such as "We lose 15 percent of our talent a year," "We're constantly orienting and training replacements," or "An employee who left last year took a key customer, and we lost a $50,000 contract." The gaps between future and current states become quite clear.

Help the team identify obstacles to achieving the desired future state, such as managers who are ill equipped to be retention managers, the lack of a retention mindset in the organization, or no development or career management programs. Finally, have the team brainstorm a long list of potential strategies for closing the gaps.

Step 5: Conduct Focus Groups and Interviews

Step 5 is to conduct focus groups and interviews. You might use the "future pull" approach with focus groups representing multiple levels and functions in the organization. The goal is to get input from numerous and diverse stakeholders.

You might ask these questions in either one-to-one interviews or focus groups:

- What do you feel is unique about your retention situation?
- What works for you, and what works against you?
- What is your hunch about why people stay?
- Tell us a story about one person who left recently. How did it happen? What did it cost in money and other losses? Could anything have been done to prevent it?
- What keeps *you* from leaving?

Step 6: Compile and Present Data

Step 6 is to compile and present data. Use all the information from your turnover and exit interview assessments, the line management belief surveys, the senior team meeting, and all focus groups and interviews. Give the senior team feedback, and present recommendations for the next steps.

While conducting your diagnosis and beginning to design retention strategies, you may want to consider putting some ongoing support structures in place. Two such structures are a retention champion and a retention task force. Either one will help you make your retention process more sustainable.

Step 7: Tap a Retention/Engagement Champion

Step 7 is to tap a retention/engagement champion. As the retention dilemma grows, it's important to craft a new job position and place someone in charge of designing ongoing retention strategies. This retention champion (typically a learning function professional) would have the primary and ongoing goal of addressing retention issues and implementing a variety of solutions, depending on the needs of various client groups. The more this person can interface with other, cross-silo, professionals such as recruiters, coaches, and trainers, the better. And the more access he or she has to line managers as well as individual contributors, the more effective the retention champion will be.

An organization might appoint rotating retention champions in all departments or a retention tribunal made up of three key champions representing the retention issues of individual contributors, supervisors, and midlevel managers.

Step 8: Prepare Managers to Become Owners

Step 8 is to prepare managers to become owners. The learning and development leader is vital in this step. Managers often have the will, but not the skill, to engage and retain their talented performers.

Start by asking "Who's in charge?" Until you see line managers as the owners of the retention/engagement issue, they won't see themselves that way. They'll continue to point the finger at senior management and at you. They'll continue to abdicate their role and accountability for the talent that wanders out the door, costing the company thousands or millions of dollars every year.

Acknowledge that anyone who manages someone is ultimately responsible for hanging onto that critical organizational asset. How do you do that? Show managers the research about what keeps people.

They'll quickly notice that many of the items are within their influence or control. They'll see that it's not just about money. Show them the numbers—what it costs to lose one talented member of their team. If anything sparks interest in line managers, it's finding a way to improve the bottom line.

Managers need help evaluating their strengths and weaknesses vis-à-vis retention and engagement. They also need skill training, practical strategies, and often a "tune-up" and reminders to do simple things, such as showing respect, listening, and rewarding their talent. Remind them: If they don't have time for those things, how will they find the time to recruit, interview, select, orient, and train their talented employees' replacements? Learning professionals must design solutions that build managerial skills for (1) focusing on development, (2) building relationships, and (3) creating an environment that is conducive to innovation and creativity.

Step 9: Prepare Employees to Take Responsibility for Their Own Engagement

Step 9 is to prepare employees at all levels to take responsibility for their own engagement. Most learning and development professionals recognize that individuals can and must step up to the plate and move the needle on their own workplace satisfaction. Help your crucial workers carefully consider what they want and need to stay committed and engaged at work. The more the engagement conversation is a two-way collaboration, the more effective and lasting the solution will be.

Step 10: Build Evaluation and Accountability Systems

Finally, step 10 is to build evaluation and accountability systems. As with any good organizational process or program, it's essential to stop along the way and evaluate how things are going. Is the task force working? What about the sponsorship of the senior team? Is the retention champion the right role or the right person? If any answer is *no*, it's time to go back to the drawing board.

What about accountability? Are your line managers held responsible for selecting and keeping talented people on their teams? If they lost a $10,000 piece of equipment, wouldn't they have to answer to someone? Hold them accountable for losing people assets worth that much and more. We know of a CEO who charged $30,000 to a manager's operating budget because he needlessly allowed a talented person to leave. Now that's what we call holding someone accountable.

We're not suggesting that managers should be punished when their people are promoted or move on to learn something new. It's inevitable that you'll lose some talented employees, especially as they pursue their career dreams. But we do recommend that managers be held accountable for being good retention managers and for creating a retention culture—an environment where people feel motivated, cared about, and rewarded.

In Good Times and Bad

Effective talent management, with a focus on engaging and retaining the best people, has indeed become a core business initiative. Why? Because it is abundantly clear that organizational success in *any* economy depends on excellent leadership, superior knowledge, and ongoing learning. We know now that the organizations best able to capture, engage, develop, and retain talent will flourish and succeed over the long term. And a carefully crafted, sustainable talent management process ensures that success.

For the past decade, we've watched managers use a talent-focused approach to building loyal, committed, productive teams. And all this is happening in an era when some said (incorrectly) that loyalty was dead. Their employees cannot be enticed away by a 10 percent raise, or a gym, or a massage on Fridays. They *love* their jobs, their teams, their bosses, and, yes, their companies. And because of this, their companies win.

In contrast, we've seen managers lose talent the moment the economy lights come back on. These not-so-successful managers matched their engagement and retention efforts to economic highs and lows. In good times, when jobs were plentiful and talented people had choices, managers offered perks, praise, and promotions.

In bad times, these leaders developed a cavalier attitude about their employees. Many felt—and some actually said—"Quit whining; be glad you have a job." They piled on the work, removed the praise, and froze the pay. Their best people readied their résumés, logged on to Monster .com, and waited for the first chance to jump ship. And the managers were stunned when it happened.

Dr. Phil, television's popular psychologist, would say to those managers, "So how did that work for you?" Not so well.

An effective approach to engaging and retaining talent is not something you turn on and off, syncing to the latest economic blip and the corresponding concern about keeping talent. It works best when it's an integrated part of your talent management practices, when it's authentic and perennial, and when you clearly believe in it, invest in it, and demonstrate it daily in your interactions with the people you want on your team.

About the Authors

Beverly Kaye is an internationally recognized authority on career issues and retention and engagement in the workplace. She was named a "Legend" by ASTD. She has also been named by *Leadership Excellence* as one of North America's 100 top thought leaders. As founder and CEO of Career Systems International and a bestselling author on workplace performance, she has worked with a host of organizations to establish cutting-edge, award-winning talent development solutions. Her first book, *Up Is Not the Only Way* (Davies Black) became a classic, and although it was published in the early 1980s, is still relevant today. In it, she foresaw the effects that leaner, flatter organizations would have on individual careers and the subsequent need for workers to take charge of their own careers. She also developed systems for leaders and employees to work together to help employees achieve their developmental goals.

Sharon Jordan-Evans, president of the Jordan Evans Group, is a pioneer in the field of employee retention and engagement. She has a master's degree in organization development and is a professionally certified coach. She serves as a speaker for numerous conferences and works with Fortune 500 companies such as American Express, Boeing, Disney, Lockheed, Cheesecake Factory, Monster, MTV, PBS, Sony, and Universal Studios. She also serves as a resource for a number of national media, including *Chief Executive*, *CIO*, *Harvard Management Update*, *Working Woman*, *Investor's Business Daily*, and the *Los Angeles Times*.

Kaye and Jordan-Evans have coauthored two *Wall Street Journal* bestsellers. The first, *Love 'Em or Lose 'Em: Getting Good People to Stay*, is the world's bestselling employee retention book and has been translated into 20 languages. The second, *Love It, Don't Leave It: 26 Ways to Get What You Want at Work*, offers easy-to-implement strategies for increasing job satisfaction and has been translated into 15 languages.

13

Engagement at 3M: A Case Study

Karen B. Paul and Cindy L. Johnson

In tough times, companies increasingly focus on the need to cut costs and be efficient. The goal is to get more done with less. Yet what if instead of cutting programs or focusing on which HR processes could be streamlined and enhanced for better efficiency, HR professionals focused on just optimizing across their entire function? This is essentially the idea behind integrated talent solutions at 3M, a global technology company, which seeks improvement in integration across its HR processes.

Although the idea of integrated talent solutions is relatively simple, its execution is anything but easy. Instead of deliverables from each HR function, the goal becomes delivering integrated solutions for clients. This was essentially the challenge Angela S. Lalor, senior vice president of human resources, gave to the Talent Development and Organizational Effectiveness organization at 3M in 2006. This is the story of how 3M's human resource function more tightly integrated all of its services through the use of employee engagement and how learning and development came to be the major focal point for the integration.

Aligning HR Processes With the Business Strategy

If HR processes are aligned with the corporate-wide business strategy, integration across HR processes is simpler to achieve. In 3M's case, this meant enhancing innovation through employee engagement.

Throughout the twentieth century, 3M had an unsurpassed record of breakthrough innovation and bringing new products to markets, earning its place as a Fortune 500 company and frequently appearing on lists of most admired companies. But in 2006, the company was struggling to keep its momentum in driving efficiency gains while reaffirming its commitment to radical innovation.

To meet these challenges, 3M decided to leverage its existing high levels of employee engagement and use engagement as a tool to boost creativity and efficiency simultaneously. Its top management team worked with HR executives to develop corporate and business unit plans to help the company achieve the balance it needed between increased creativity to feed the pipeline of radically new products, on one hand, and the efficiency it needed to turn new ideas into new products and bring them to market at the highest speed and lowest cost possible, on the other hand. To be successful, employees at all levels must be actively engaged or the objectives of developing new products and reviewing existing products and processes to help customers will fall short of expectations.

By taking a different and more consistent approach to employee engagement since 2006, 3M has capitalized on its past successes and improved business performance. It has found that engagement is the key to balancing creativity and efficiency, freedom, and discipline. Its renewed focus on employee engagement has allowed it to boost innovation without losing momentum in its drive to efficiency.

Providing a Unifying Framework and Measurement

As part of the initial rollout, 3M instituted a common worldwide definition and measurement of engagement for all its employees. It defines employee engagement as "an individual's sense of purpose and focused energy, evident to others in the display of personal initiative, effort, and persistence directed toward *organizational goals*." This definition provided not only a common language and framework for employees to learn about engagement, but also the foundation for ways to bring various HR services together to deliver for the businesses. This common definition also allowed for the measurement of perceptions of engagement.

3M has been actively measuring employee attitudes about the workplace since 1951. In 2007, it also started to measure its level of employee engagement. The survey assesses the conditions for engagement, employee perceptions on issues ranging from job challenges to fairness, the relationship with managers and other employees, and actual levels of engagement itself. It also looks at the alignment between the company's aims and employees' aims.

The survey is global and standardized throughout the company. This allows 3M to benchmark its results against those of other companies. Standardization provides the basis for the survey to be used as a data-gathering exercise. The data allows for comparisons at the local, divisional, and company levels and provides the basis for developing strategic tools to help the company achieve its goals at these same levels. Further, by providing a baseline measurement of employee engagement, subsequent progress on plans can be tracked and reported.

The objective for this effort is twofold: to create a corporate-wide plan to provide overall education, training, and development on employee engagement and to provide support to the business units to enable them to take action on the concepts communicated in and through the corporate-wide components of the strategy.

Using Leadership Development as the Catalyst for Change

3M started its engagement journey by building the fundamental concepts into its leadership classes worldwide. For subsequent innovation to emerge, it is critical that leaders create the conditions for engagement. 3M views engagement as essentially a leadership responsibility, and as such, leadership development would become a key for success. By leveraging its leadership development programs, 3M was able to educate leaders not only on the conceptual portion of employee engagement, but also to provide practical advice. While a leader is teaching, he or she can provide stronger linkages between leadership (as defined) and how it translates into specific behaviors.

The cornerstone of 3M's leadership development programs is the concept of leaders teaching leaders. Senior executives teach other executives, which in practice is an engagement exercise in itself. The leaders quickly learn which practices are the most successful with other leaders. The process of leaders teaching leaders also provides a model for participants on how to engage people. Leaders also share their own individual success stories and their approaches to engagement.

Action learning is another key component of 3M's leadership development programs. In action learning, participants, whether in the company's Accelerated Leadership Development Program or Emerging Leaders Program, are charged with a business problem to solve with a group of other participants. Typically, each group is given about 10 days to solve their problem. Conclusions of the projects are reported back and debriefed in front of the CEO and those who report directly to him as part of the last day of the experience.

The CEO also sets an example by teaching in 3M's Leadership Development Institute. This modeling by example has led 3M senior executives to take very seriously their roles as teachers in 3M leadership programs. The CEO is also an active mentor and has all top executives serve as mentors in a formal program. Each executive has two mentees for a one-year period, with an emphasis on diversity.

Feedback from 3M's leadership development programs also provides reciprocal loop learning for human resources both in terms of future topics that should be covered as well as how seamlessly HR processes are working to provide solutions. 3M's leadership development programs have been honored with both *Fortune*'s 2009–10 Global and North American Top Companies for Leaders and *CEO Magazine*'s 2009 Best Companies for Leaders.

Most recently, leadership development staff have been raising the bar on their own award-winning approach. In the nine years that 3M has offered the Accelerated Leadership Development Program (ALDP), 71 action learning projects were successfully completed during 23 sessions.

Participants and experts outside the company have recognized the program as highly successful on a number of fronts. To adapt the program so that it connects to the new Emerging Leaders Program, the following changes were made for 2010:

- Each action learning project will have an economic goal of at least $25 million in new sales. This goal will be achieved without reducing existing international growth plans or division strategic plans.

- Action learning project recommendations will be implemented by subsidiary operations in growing economies.

- Participants from the Emerging Leaders Program will be expected to contribute at least 15 percent of their time during the year following the session to achieve the results, coordinate with sponsors, and transfer relevant knowledge within the company.

These changes help cultivate the growth mindset of 3M's subsidiary leaders and to achieve the company's leadership development objectives. Typically, an ALDP team has 60 to 70 hours to develop and recommend a solution to the CEO, operations committee, and sponsors, after which the sponsor is left to resource and implement the plan. Under the new approach, ALDP teams create the global direction and strategic intent for their projects. The results from the projects become the starting point for the action leaning projects in the Emerging Leaders Program.

The new Emerging Leaders Program is designed to address the issue of rapid growth and how to maximize 3M's capabilities worldwide. For the first session, participants are from three global regions: Central Eastern Europe, the Middle East and Africa, and Latin America.

The emerging leaders have 50 to 60 hours of action learning in which to build a plan to implement or alter the ALDP project recommendations in their region or country. Those plans are then reviewed for resource approval by the area vice presidents. After the program is completed, the participants will be expected to work approximately 15 percent of their time during the next 12 months implementing their plans. Additionally, there would be two or three review meetings when the emerging leaders group in the three global regions would report their lessons and results to their executive sponsors.

This change has created a very exciting and challenging learning experience, and the monetary goal has raised the stakes for both senior executives and participants alike. Action learning projects are now enjoying their highest scores since their inception in 2001. Commentary from leaders participating and teaching reflects the highest level of engagement, with class scores moving from 4.68 to 4.82 on a scale of 1 to 5, with 5 being the most engaged. Leadership development at 3M has become a catalyst for change and engagement.

Providing Education and Tools

Another prominent component of 3M's support for engagement is education. 3M deploys learning modules delivered in traditional classroom settings as well as utilizing intranet-based training. As part of the initial rollout, 3M trained HR employees worldwide on engagement and provided a tool kit for HR business partners to use with their organizations to improve engagement.

For example, one item in the tool kit is the employment value tool. This tool is a discussion guide for supervisors, which supervisors are then trained to use, to help them discuss with their employees what areas and types of work are most engaging. The discussion is voluntary on the part of the employee and begins with the employees completing a form that they deliver to their supervisors before the discussion. The process is optional. Then, based on the information in the form, the manager holds a discussion with the employee. The discussion focuses on the employee's view of his or her current work and position, development opportunities, compensation, benefits, management and work environment, and a variety of other factors. The outcome of this discussion helps a supervisor better understand the individual's wants and needs, what motivates them, and how best to engage each employee.

To further educate supervisors, a series of engagement videos were created. Each video is no more than 10 minutes in length. The purpose of the video is to elaborate on an important component of engagement.

Topics have ranged from the business case for engagement to the importance of trust, especially during hard economic times. Angela Lalor, senior VP of human resources, introduces and positions each video. A typical video highlights a senior executive providing a point of view on the topic followed by a subject matter expert providing a skill-building component.

3M also uses social media to educate employees. In fact, 3M has used social media extensively (for example, DIY Video—a YouTube-like internal video posting system, blogs, wikis, and an internal social networking site). A recent employee engagement video contest helped to unleash the creative energies of employees and provided new tools and techniques for creating new patterns of communication and also as a method for engaging employees. The purpose of the video contest was to encourage the use of social media within the company and to provide video footage that could be used for elaborating on key messages such as employee engagement for 3M. Several winning entries can be seen on the 3M Careers Facebook page. 3M has found that engagement and leadership development are key topics of interest among many new recruits and that the video contest was a fun method of providing information and giving applicants an insider's view of both employee engagement and 3M.

Aligning HR Processes to Deliver Solutions

A company that develops and hopes to maintain a culture of innovation must actively manage and engage talent at all levels. At the core of 3M's Human Resource Principles is "respect for people," which provides a strong, solid foundation for talent processes. The 3M Human Resource Principles are

- Respect the dignity and worth of individuals, by encouraging their highest level of performance in a fair, challenging, objective, and cooperative work environment. Individual rights are respected. Timely and open communication to and from employees is encouraged. Supervisors and managers are accountable for the performance and development of the employees assigned to them.

- Encourage the initiative of each employee by providing both direction and the freedom to work creatively. Risk taking and innovation are requirements for growth. Both are to be encouraged and supported in an atmosphere of integrity and mutual respect.

- Challenge individual capabilities through proper placement, orientation, and development. Responsibility for development is shared by the employee, by supervisors and managers, and by the company.

- Provide equal opportunity for development and equitably reward good performance. Performance is evaluated against objective job-related criteria and is rewarded with appropriate recognition and compensation.

3M also changed its Leadership Attributes to underscore the importance of employee engagement as a leadership responsibility. The 3M Leadership Attributes are

- Make courageous decisions.
- Think from the outside in.
- Drive innovation and growth.
- Develop, teach, and *engage* others.
- Lead with energy, passion, and urgency.
- Live 3M values.

3M's Leadership Attributes serve as the common thread aligning its HR processes and practices. The Leadership Attributes serve as the foundation for all of 3M's upper-level leadership development courses. As part of these courses, leaders participate in a 360-degree process whereby they are given feedback and coaching on the Leadership Attributes. There is also a 360-degree process available to all employees that provides feedback on the Leadership Attributes and advice and guidance for a development plan based on the scores. In 3M's talent development process, leaders are identified through the businesses during management team reviews, which review individuals as part of the performance management cycle. Before these meetings, individuals self-define their contributions in terms of what they delivered versus what they committed to deliver. During the consensus management team review, there is also an assessment of the individual's leadership attributes.

To get a cross-sectional look at talent, 3M instituted functional (or tier) reviews. Here all employees belonging to a functional grouping (for example, engineering, or R&D) are reviewed regardless of their business unit to get a functional perspective on the organization and talent.

These various assessments roll into the "Health of the Organization" process, where more factors are calibrated, including further development and reward and recognition. All the information from these processes feeds succession planning. Each month, the CEO holds reviews of talent and placements. Twice a year, during the "Health of the Organization" process, he personally reviews each business's talent pipeline with them and reviews how they are developing talent.

3M's talent mindset also helps it maintain a balance between current human capital needs and those of the changing market. To do this, the company seeks to strike a careful balance between developing people within the corporation and attracting new and experienced talent from outside the company. New innovations and business strategies can often be most quickly realized with existing internal talent. In other situations, specific knowledge needs may make external talent the approach of choice. A connection to the business strategy and a knowledge of the talent needs and talent capabilities of the particular business unit are critical to engaging all essential talent.

The company has always relied heavily upon employee engagement. Innovation, arguably 3M's most treasured asset, rests upon and is fueled by employee engagement. New employees at 3M quickly learn of the expectations around involvement and taking action. Thus, it was natural for 3M to treat employee engagement as part of the innovation process—something powered by concerned employees working to solve customer challenges.

Management plays a big role in engaging employees and giving them the best opportunity to innovate. Through employee engagement, management makes sure that the aims of the firm and those of its employees are aligned. They encourage risk taking. They reassure employees that innovation is a priority, that they have the support and backing of executive management, and that failure will be tolerated. They cultivate trust in management through timely and meaningful feedback and discussion and by rewarding employees for taking risks and for success in bringing new products to market, by giving them cash rewards, status elevations, or promotions, according to what managers feel will be the most valued.

But ultimately, innovation comes from engaged employees who are able and willing to put their best effort, passion, and energy into creating new products, thus actively seeking feedback from customers, networking with peers within and outside the firm, seeking more experienced mentors, taking the time to "tinker," showing resilience and persistence when faced with early failures, and taking risks.

HR's job at 3M is to facilitate the integration of the firm's business processes and practices to ensure that its culture is one that sustains engagement and innovation over time. At 3M, managing and engaging talent isn't an annual "event" but a continuous process, composed of various integrated subprocesses, evaluations, and tools.

About the Authors

Karen B. Paul is manager of HR measurement, talent solutions, at 3M. Previously, she was the talent manager for several of 3M's global big businesses. Before joining 3M, she was manager of research and development at NCS Pearson. Her articles have been published in the *Journal of Applied Psychology* and *T+D*, and her work on employee engagement was profiled as a best practice case by the Conference Board. She co-wrote the chapter "Selection in Multinational Corporations" in the *Handbook of Employee Selection* (with Paula Caligiuri; Erlbaum, 2010). She received her PhD in industrial and organizational psychology from Bowling Green State University.

Cindy L. Johnson is director of talent development, talent solutions, 3M. The focus of her work is designing and building accelerated global talent development programs for 3M's future leaders. She conceptualized and developed the Leadership Continuum, a career-long growth process for 3M employees through the executive levels based on global leadership competencies. And she recently completed a two-year project managing the design and building of 3M's new Leadership Development Institute. She has more than 25 years' experience in executive and global leadership development, employee development programs, and facility management.

Section VII

■ ■ ■

Leadership Development

Global Leadership Development

Noel M. Tichy

An organization that develops leaders at all levels gains a competitive advantage in today's global, increasingly knowledge-based economy. At the end of the last century, leaders won with brains, not brawn. Thus, in developing leadership, the dependent variable is honing leaders' judgment capacity. In our book *Judgment*, Warren Bennis and I conclude that the essential genome of leadership is judgment. To make good leadership judgments, leaders need to develop skill and knowledge in three fundamental areas:

- *People*—deciding who is on the team or off the team and how to develop those who are on the team.
- *Strategy*—deciding what direction to take the organization.
- *Crises*—dealing with the inevitable crises that all organizations face.

Figure 14-1 illustrates a framework for leadership development based on the process of enabling the leader to hone his or her capacity to make judgments. We argue that like medical doctors in training, leaders only really learn in a clinical practice—by actually making real judgments. This is why residency programs for young doctors are built around making clinical judgments. Even though a resident can make life-changing judgments, the residency framework does include some safety nets. Senior resident leaders and the head of residency provide continuous coaching and feedback. In the analogous case of action learning in companies, we create the equivalent of a residency program by giving teams of leaders real projects with real consequences, requiring the application and development of good business acumen, good leadership, and teamwork. To provide safety nets, the CEO frames and guides each project, and each team also has a senior leader coach and sponsor. Projects require both leaders and team members to follow good leadership judgment, as outlined in figure 14-1. The process of good judgment is the same whether the judgment concerns people, strategy, or a crisis. Because judgment is a clinical skill, it requires real clinical practice and feedback.

Figure 14-1. The Importance of Following Good Leadership Judgment During All Project Phases

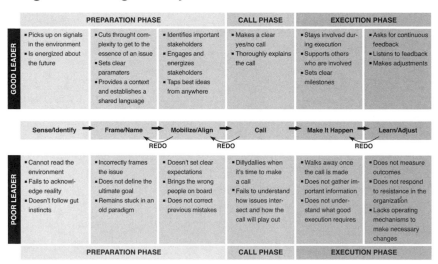

Source: Tichy and Bennis, 2007.

This framework guides leadership development at all levels. For example, as a consultant at Best Buy, I worked with the store managers, who then tasked the young staff in the stores with defining the value propositions for customers, with teaching each other, running real-time experiments, reviewing daily profit and loss statements for their stores, making adjustments, and engaging in the critical process of hiring and firing colleagues. The goal was to develop good leadership judgment at the front line to drive performance and develop field-tested leaders.

At the associate level, the developing leaders needed to do a good job in the preparation phase by identifying emerging customer trends and needs, framing and naming the judgment that needed to be made, and then aligning key stakeholders to set up the call phase. The execution phase is equally important. At Best Buy, a key strategic judgment was the acquisition and growth of the Geek Squad to do home installations and provide computer services. Associates at the floor level saw the need and helped frame the judgment for the CEO, Brad Anderson, to buy the Geek Squad company and make it a part of Best Buy to support home installation and computer servicing. The execution phase was supported by an action learning project in 2002 that focused on how to better integrate services in the stores and grow the service business. This is now a multibillion-dollar Best Buy business. For another pertinent story that provides a framework for the discussion that follows, see the sidebar.

Historical Context: Action Learning as an Evolutionary Journey

In the early 1970s, as a faculty member at Columbia University's Graduate School of Business, I launched an executive program, Organization Development and Human Resources Management, based on an action learning model—so students could work on real change projects while developing as leaders. When I moved to the University of Michigan, I launched the Advanced Human Resource Management Program in 1981, which was an action learning, three-workshop platform for human resource leaders to lead transformations in their companies. This led to the creation of action learning programs at companies including Honeywell, Exxon, and Whirlpool, before I took over as head of GE's fabled leadership center, Crotonville, in 1985. That experience set the stage for working with other global companies including Mercedes-

Benz, Intuit, Royal Dutch Shell, Nokia, Numera Securities, Best Buy, Walmart, Pepsi, Ford, Mexico's Grupo Salinas, and Thailand's CP, among others, to design and build world-class leadership development. I have also worked with the Navy SEALS, hospitals, and school systems as they build their leadership pipelines. Surprising to some, the fundamentals translate across cultures, industries, and sectors. Thus this sidebar provides a framework for guiding the social architecture of a robust leadership pipeline that integrates senior leadership ownership, on-the-job leadership development, and powerful leadership development programs.

GE'S Global Development Strategy: Crotonville Benchmark

General Electric's management development operation headquartered at Crotonville, New York, provides formal development experiences for GE professionals and managers worldwide. Each year, approximately 5,000 employees come to Crotonville's 53-acre campus, which has a 200-plus bed residential education center. In the mid-1980s, while I ran Crotonville in collaboration with CEO Jack Welch, we changed its mission to focus on global development. The new objective became "to leverage GE's global competitiveness as an instrument of cultural change, by improving the business acumen, leadership abilities, and organizational effectiveness of General Electric professionals."

From that point forward, Crotonville has served as a transformational lever for GE, as well as an individual leadership development tool. Therefore, many of the premises that guided CEO Jack Welch's actions in the 1980s have generalized applicability to transnational companies around the world. The GE case illustrates how the training and development infrastructure of large companies can serve to bring about much more compressed, higher-impact change than currently experienced. Such global change will require that CEOs have a new mindset, similar to the one that Welch developed. He grasped that winning globally requires continuous employee development at all levels, ensuring that GE develops a culture in which the need for speed, continuous experimentation, and action is met.

Welch perceived himself to be a leader of a major cultural revolution at GE. He had been looking for ways to best utilize GE's Crotonville resources. In keeping with this imperative, one of the fundamental premises guiding the transformation of Crotonville during the 1980s was that revolutionaries do not rely solely on the chain of command to catalyze quantum change. They carefully develop multichannel, two-way, interactive networks throughout the organization:

- The chain of command, with its vested interest, is where much of the resistance to change resides. Therefore, there is a need to stir up the populace of the organization, to begin developing new leaders for the new regime.
- There is a need for a new set of values and templates in the organization.
- There is a need for mechanisms to implement all these changes. Therefore, new socialization and new development processes are required.

The Crotonville Transformation

Similar to most university business schools, the primary focus at Crotonville had historically been on the individual participant's cognitive understanding. The shift in the Crotonville mindset has been from a training mentality to a workshop mentality, which ultimately leads to a completely new program design. It has resulted in a greater number of teams attending sessions whenever possible. Also, participants increasingly bring real business problems to the table and leave with real action plans.

Before going to Crotonville, participants' individual leadership behaviors are rated by their direct reports, peers, and bosses. The aim is for changes in leadership behavior to be linked back to the work setting. Other action learning tools include having executives consult real GE businesses on unresolved strategic issues. Teams spend up to a week in the field consulting with these businesses. In addition, members of the CEO's team and officers come to Crotonville to conduct workshops on key GE strategic challenges.

Along the way, participants find the development experiences increasingly unsettling and emotionally charged. They experience discomfort with the feedback from their back-home organization. They wrestle with very difficult, unresolved, real-life problems. They make presentations to senior executives, argue among themselves, and work through intensive team-building experiences that include a good deal of Outward Bound–type activity. The measure of program success shifts from participants' evaluation of how good they felt about the learning experience to how the experience has affected their organizations and their own leadership behavior over time.

For the Crotonville program to deliver on its new global mission in the 1980s, the total curriculum was revamped to provide a targeted "core development" experience at key career transition points for people at all levels—from new professional hires up through the top management offices.

Figure 14-2 shows the core dimensions necessary for reframing development challenges. This figure illustrates the depth of the training solution. As solutions like these become deeper, leaders move from a focus on developing (1) awareness and (2) cognitive and conceptual understanding to (3) actual skills, (4) new problem-solving approaches, and ultimately to (5) fundamental change. The level of risk goes up at each stage. More time is required to develop the deeper training solution.

The other dimension in figure 14-2 is the focus (or target) of the training solution, with one end of the spectrum being anchored at the individual level and the other at the organizational level. Traditional programs commonly send individuals either to internal management development programs or to external business school programs. Occasionally, boss–subordinate pairs or two colleagues attend programs. Less rarely, but still part of the repertoire of traditional development programs,

Figure 14-2. The Core Dimensions Needed to Reframe Development Challenges

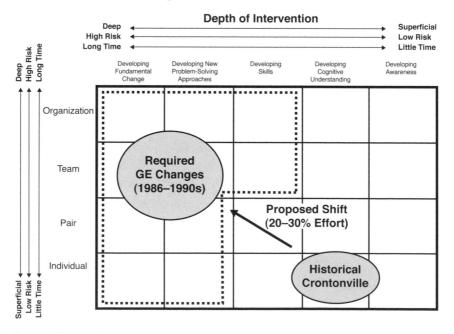

Source: Tichy and Sherman, 1993.

teams are sent, and finally, the target is sometimes the total organization. In contrast, the development matrix shown in figure 14-2 asserts that the challenge is to move development toward the upper left portion of the matrix, "developing fundamental change."

Guidelines for Linking Development With Reality

When management development programs are reconceptualized as action workshops, real "live" problems, not case studies, command attention. People in the action experience are at real risk, and there are tangible organizational goals for transformation that are linked to the development activities. Add globalization to the agenda, and the model for successful compressed action learning becomes clear: intense cross-culture problem solving that requires multicultural teams, a faculty that is transcultural as well as multilingual, and breaking free of the classroom into real cross-cultural settings. Only when these cross-cultural teams of executives are *required to deliver* with *real* stakes and *real* risks involved, can there be a quantum development breakthrough.

As organizations compete on the global playing field of the 21st century, competitive leaders at all levels rise to a new level. The lessons learned in the past 20 years have led to the development of five guidelines for building the competitive leadership pipeline of the future. Leadership development is both on the job as well as in special programs. Thus there needs to be an integration of leadership development and overall talent and succession management that follows these five guidelines:

- Articulate a teachable point of view.
- Embrace the 80/20 rule.
- Utilize action learning.
- Move from the top down.
- Build the rest of the leadership development institute.

Let's look briefly at each guideline.

The First Guideline: Articulate a Teachable Point of View

The first guideline is to articulate a teachable point of view. The CEO and the top management team need to clearly articulate a teachable point of view for how the organization will succeed in the future. This includes the need to clearly articulate ideas (a global business strategy) and a set of values (how all employees need to behave to support the ideas; a set of assumptions about how to emotionally energize all employees by using rewards and consequences) and the ability to exercise yes/no judgments about people, strategy, and crises consistent with the ideas and values of the company. This teachable point of view must be embedded at all levels by leaders teaching leaders, not by outsourcing teaching to consultants and professors.

An example of this is Brad Anderson, who, when he was CEO of Best Buy, worked with the top management team to change the strategy from commodity, low-cost, volume selling of consumer electronics to a customer-centric model. The teachable point of view required new strategic ideas to segment the customer base, to identify key segments, and to develop clear value propositions for how to make money in major segments, such as high-end customers, female customers, and small business customers. This further required a new set of values for working with customers in the store, such as empowering store associates with the tools and freedom to solve customer needs. This teachable point of view was then made the framework for using an action learning platform to reach all 100,000 associates.

The Second Guideline: Embrace the 80/20 Rule

The second guideline is that the 80/20 rule must be embraced by the leadership. Because 80 percent of leadership development is on-the-job and life experience, designing career paths to build leaders is a critical task of senior leadership. Cross-functional, cross-cultural, and cross-business experiences with coaching, learning, and assessment at all stages are critical. The 20 percent that can be influenced by formal development needs to be extraordinarily effective, and thus the dial is turned up very high on action learning—for real projects with real results.

At GE, the 80/20 rule was tied to succession planning at all levels. The leadership team gave careful consideration to assignments of leaders for both the sake of the business and the development of the leader. Specific development agendas were articulated for leaders as they moved into new assignments, and they were tracked and reviewed systematically.

To implement the 80/20 rule at GE, we followed the set of guidelines shown in figure 14-3, the leadership pipeline audit, which highlights the important elements in building the leadership pipeline infrastructure in a company.

Figure 14-3. Leadership Pipeline Audit

Leader identification

	Score				
	Not at all				Definitely
1. There are at least three viable contenders for each senior position on the team.	1	2	3	4	5
2. Our leadership pipeline screens leaders for their Teachable Point of View.	1	2	3	4	5
3. The leaders who are contenders to move up have demonstrated that the can develop other leaders behind them by creating Virtuous Teaching Cycles.	1	2	3	4	5

Pipeline architecture

4. Deliberate development opportunities are created at each career stage.	1	2	3	4	5
5. We have identified competencies and values required of future leaders, not those of the past.	1	2	3	4	5
6. There is deliberate effort to ensure that leaders have a broad base of experience to understand the business (across geography, business unit, P&L capability, etc.).	1	2	3	4	5

Source: Tichy and Cardwell, 2002.

To guide succession planning at GE, Jack Welch personally led an effort to define the leadership pipeline. When I was running Crotonville, GE's leadership institute, Welch had my colleague, Don Kane, and I work with him and then–vice chairman, Larry Bossidy, to articulate what leadership characteristics were going to be needed in the future. Welch said, "However I got to be CEO is irrelevant: The world has changed, our values have changed, we need to create leaders for tomorrow's world." We spent more than 18 months with Welch and Bossidy discussing, debating, and agreeing upon what we wanted in the way of leadership characteristics across all of GE's businesses anywhere in the world, whether Jet Engines, Medical Systems, or Capital. We incorporated interpersonal skills, functional/product skills, and organizational skills. Table 14-1 presents a summary of the framework.

This framework provided Welch, the CEO, as well as the heads of the businesses and the human resource staff with a template for position assignments. It was used in succession planning discussions throughout the company.

Developing a leadership pipeline for the company is not a consultant or staff activity; it is a CEO responsibility and needs to be done regularly as the world changes. The same fundamental process was used at Best Buy, Intuit, and Shell. It is not industry specific: It is a thoughtful, disciplined, strategic talent planning process.

The Third Guideline: Utilize Action Learning

The third guideline is to utilize action learning. Action learning entails simultaneous leadership development and work to solve real problems. If done right, you get $1 + 1 = 4$:

1 [leadership development] + 1 [task force] = 4

(twice the impact on leadership development and twice the impact on task force results)

With action learning, there is better leadership development due to feedback based on the leader's regular job, 360-degree feedback before the start of the program, and improvement plans and feedback from teammates during the action learning program, complete with rigorous

Table 14-1. A Leadership Development Framework Using Action Learning to Reach All Employees

Employee	Interpersonal Skills	Functional/Product Skills	Organizational Skills
Individual contributor	Build effective communication and relationship skills Effectively deal with personal strengths and weaknesses	Develop specific functional skills Learn roles and relationships within the functional/product unit Develop work planning, programming, and performance assessment skills	Reconcile personal values with organizational value system Understand how his/her function and business relates to the entire company Grasp role of the company in the global marketplace Learn about customers and suppliers
New manager	Learn to delegate work and get things done through other people Learn to effectively appraise the performance of subordinates and secure their improved performance Acquire and effectively apply team-building skills Learn to share insights and values with others so that effect is multiplied	Acquire basic managerial skills, such as budgeting or program planning	Reconcile personal values with company's shared values Learn to integrate work of unit with related units

Table 14-1. A Leadership Development Framework Using Action Learning to Reach All Employees, continued

Experienced manager	Develop negotiation skills and effectiveness in dealing with conflict situations Gain executive communication skills required for broad-scale communications Increase ability to deal with ambiguity, paradox, and situations where there is not a single "right" answer	Gain deep, well-rounded understanding of all related functional skills in area of prime assignment	Develop strategic thinking skills and the capacity to use both inductive and deductive problem solving Learn how to effectively implement organizational change Understand the difference between what is best for the customer and what is easiest for the business Maximize understanding of global business dynamics and interfunctional relationships
General manager	Gain capacity to deal concurrently with multiple issues of increasing complexity and ambiguity Develop a recognition that he or she cannot and should not try to solve all problems personally Build skill in framing problems for others to solve Understand how to maximize contributions of individual, team, and staff Develop a recognition that asking for help is a sign of maturity rather than a weakness Develop the sensitivity to respond to the needs of others based on limited stimulus or cues		Refine broad perspective that extends to the well-being of the entire organization Sharpen analytical and critical thinking skills for organizational problem solving Play an active role in the development of the vision for his or her business

Business leader	Learn to effectively exercise power in making those decisions that only the leader can make Develop projection and extrapolation skills to deal with situations where he or she has no firsthand knowledge Develop sensitivity to the forces that motivate people to behave as they do	Develop multifunctional integration skills to manage a business based on profit and loss Develop and effectively articulate the vision for the business Develop the capacity to conceive, not just adopt, change Develop an effective understanding of the dynamics of the industry Develop a balanced posture between leadership of the business and integration/cooperation among the functions or other businesses in the company Develop the capacity to effectively manage community relations

Source: Tichy and Cohen, 1997.

improvement plans. In the equation on page 156, the second "1," which represents the project task force, is better because it is inserted into a disciplined process led by the CEO and top management team.

The Fourth Guideline: Move From the Top Down

The fourth guideline is to move from the top down. The CEO and the top management team need to build their leadership institute from the "penthouse" down. That is, start with the CEO leading an action learning program by engaging six teams of about six senior up-and-coming leaders working on strategic projects owned and framed by the CEO and the top management team. The participants are selected and assigned to teams by the CEO and the top management team. This project and selection process typically take about a half day to a full day working with the CEO and the top management team. In addition, each team has a senior leader, a coach, and a sponsor who are just that—a coach and a sponsor, not members or leaders of the team.

Why top down? Because this approach intellectually and emotionally commits the top management team to action learning. These are strategic projects done by emerging senior leaders on topics they truly care about.

We have implemented this CEO-driven action learning program at GE Medical Systems, Numera Securities, Royal Dutch Shell, Ford, Intuit, the Royal Bank of Canada, Intel, Grupo Salinas, and CP in Thailand.

The Fifth Guideline: Build the Rest of the Leadership Development Institute

The fifth guideline is to build the rest of the leadership development institute. First you need to identify appropriate career transition points, similar to GE's pipeline, and then you can design action learning experiences appropriate to leaders at that level.

To show how these five guidelines work in practice, let's look at a very illuminating case study of action learning, the Global Leadership Program at GE.

A Case Study of Action Learning: GE's Global Leadership Program

The GE Global Leadership Program is a change process designed to speed up the company's globalization. The GLP simultaneously solves global strategic challenges while developing the global leadership and team skills of individual participants. This is accomplished through "compressed action learning."

Compressed action learning puts teams (typically six to eight six-person teams) and individuals under extreme pressure to solve real organizational problems within tight time constraints, while activity paradoxically takes place in a supportive learning environment where there is time to learn new skills and concepts, which then are immediately put into practice to solve strategic challenges.

The GLP is led by the CEO and the senior management team, whose members actively participate as coaches, project sponsors, and active participants in the commitment change process. The GLP's nine-month process starts with senior managers selecting key global projects, then selecting teams from different regions of the world (see figure 14-4). Before the first of three workshops, each selected individual goes through an extensive personal assessment as a global leader that includes having surveys filled out by six to eight colleagues on specific global leadership behaviors. Each GLP participant receives feedback on how he or she is seen by self versus how others see him or her. The first workshop lasts five days and is aimed at launching the global teams, getting the strategic projects under way, and starting the journey to develop more global mindsets and networks.

Following the first workshop, teams return to their regular jobs while simultaneously working on their global projects. There is a midcourse, three-day workshop to give help and feedback on the projects and to work on team processes, share best practices, and get coaching support.

The final step is an intensive commitment workshop. The participants work with senior managers focused on each project for a half day to review their achievements and realizations, work through the recom-

Figure 14-4. Overview of the Process for the Global Leadership Program

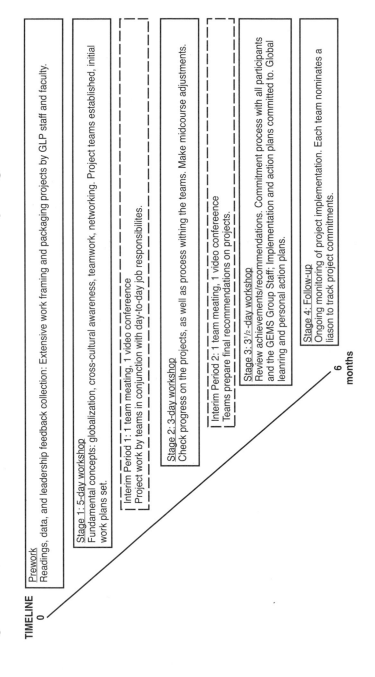

TIMELINE

Prework
Readings, data, and leadership feedback collection: Extensive work framing and packaging projects by GLP staff and faculty.

Stage 1: 5-day workshop
Fundamental concepts: globalization, cross-cultural awareness, teamwork, networking. Project teams established, initial work plans set.

Interim Period 1: 1 team meating, 1 video confereence
Project work by teams in conjunction with day-to-day job responsibilites.

Stage 2: 3-day workshop
Check progress on the projects, as well as process withing the teams. Make midcourse adjustments.

Interim Period 2: 1 team meating, 1 video confereence
Teams prepare final recommendations on projects.

Stage 3: 3¹/₂-day workshop
Review achievements/recommendations. Commitment process with all participants and the GEMS Group Staff; Implementation and action plans committed to. Global leanring and personal action plans.

Stage 4: Follow-up
Ongoing monitoring of project implementation. Each team nominates a liason to track project commitments.

0

6
months

Source: Tichy, Pucik, and Barnett, 1992.

mendations, and make real implementation commitments. In addition, time is taken to assess the "soft" human global leadership learning.

The final workshop, stage 3 in figure 14-4, has four objectives.

- Run the best global meeting ever.
- Make commitments to implement recommendations from all projects.
- Continue global individual, team, and organizational learning and development.
- Prepare for passing learning to the next GLP group of participants.

The final workshop is a change implementation meeting. The team assignments were given because they are critical to the company's global success. The leaders of the company are asked to help make change happen. Therefore, the final workshop is an opportunity to mobilize a critical mass of leadership to implement a change plan. It is designed to help get people to buy in through discussion, debate, compromise, and ultimately by commitments to implementation.

The design of the final workshop is *not* a typical "old way" company presentation. It is a "new way" high participation process for the company leaders to take ownership of all the projects (typically six to eight); see table 14-2.

Each team's written report should recommend a concrete action plan with specific steps to make change happen. The text should be no longer than 15 pages plus exhibits. The reports should include

- mission
- methodology
- analysis of issue(s)
- recommendation(s) for action (1 page)
- specific action steps: who, what, when, and so on (1 page).

The recommendation(s) should deal with the real challenge of change— the technical, political, and cultural domains. The object is to have real change happen.

Table 14-2. How the Design of the Final Workshop Is Not a Typical "Old Way" Company Presentation but a "New Way" High Participation Process

"Old Way"	"New Way"
No reports ahead of time	Written report prepared for everyone
No preparation by nonpresenting teams	Reading and preparation ahead of time
Formal "pitch"	Minimal formal "pitch"
Little debate	Thorough discussion/debate
Passive audience	Real-time modification to improve recommendations
All energy focused on the boss	Total GLP commitment and "buy-in" to make change happen
No one has ownership	Continuous learning and development

Source: Tichy, Pucik, and Barnett, 1992.

A responsibility of all GLP participants and the group staff is to read each of the reports before the presentations. It assumes that the global leaders within the company have ownership of all the GLP projects and are prepared to help with implementation.

Table 14-3 summarizes the leadership impact of the program.

The GLP is both a lever for transforming the company and a powerful leadership experience. A unique set of building blocks, or social technologies, is used in the GLP to achieve the results. There are five primary goals for the GLP:

- Deliver on the *global projects*—to make changes in the company.
- Develop *global mindsets*.
- Develop *global leadership* skills.
- Develop *global team* skills.
- Develop *global networks*.

The GLP is delivered by creating a temporary system, that is, building a social organization with its own structure, leadership, and values.

Table 14-3. Leadership Development Impact of the Global Leadership Program

Impact on the Senior Leadership Team: • *A global team-building process*—The Global Leadership Program forces teamwork through selection of projects, guidance of program, and then commitment to take action. • A tool for *developing global leadership skills*—senior leaders are tested and learn as leaders in a global context. • *Global role model*—the group is on "stage" in the final workshop—making decisions publicly and demonstrating global leadership.
Impact on the overall organization: • *GLP is an R&D lab* for new global behaviors; experimentation and learning are key to GLP. • *Global networks* are formed and reinforced across the poles of Asia, the United States, and Europe. • *Global information sharing*—best practices. • *Assessment mechanism* for succession moves. • *External viewpoints/benchmarks*—from global faculty.
Impact on individual participants: • Develop a *global mindset*—new ways of framing business power. • *Global leadership skills* practiced and developed. • *Global team skills* practiced in program.

Source: Tichy, Pucik, and Barnett, 1992.

Compressed action learning puts individuals and teams under intense time and performance pressures. They must deliver strategic change to the company while acquiring new skills and immediately use them to deliver on the projects.

One problem I uncovered at Crotonville, and was aware of for years looking at business school executive programs, was what I call the plug-in module approach. In a four-week executive program in most universities and corporate universities, one day might be spent on strategy, another on finance, marketing, team building, leadership, and so on. These modules often stand alone and are not connected to application. This is akin to a medical student taking chemistry, biology, physiology, and so forth in medical school and only combining that knowledge when the student becomes a resident making real clinical judgments.

Action learning is a platform for learning multiple lessons over time about self, leadership, teamwork, and organizational acumen while applying them along the way in solving real-life problems. One reason for the six-month process is that the projects can be much more robust, giving time for benchmarking and working with key constituencies. It also provides another learning platform—overload. We use the action learning platform, which adds 25 percent above and beyond the participant's regular job, as a way to teach and coach time management and delegation. Participants receive coaching from their regular bosses as well as the sponsor and faculty.

At each stage, action learning appropriate to the level is used as the developmental driver. For example, at GE we had a three-day workshop for 2,000 mostly young engineers. They came to learn about global competition, GE's strategy, GE's values, and how to get their careers off to a fast start as individual contributors. They had to come to Crotonville with an improvement project to which their bosses had agreed, such as quality improvement or a work process improvement. As you move up the hierarchy, projects get broader and broader, but they all have the same criteria—importance to the organization at that level, being jointly owned with the boss, and having measurable consequences—or else they fail the reality test.

The identifiable teachable moments portrayed in figure 14-5 are typical of the careers of the leaders in most large organizations. They start with new hires, where there is an opportunity to imprint the company's values and culture as well as fundamental work skills. For first-time leaders, there is an opportunity to imprint on them as they transition from being individual contributors to leaders of other people. Key elements are how to hire, appraise, develop, build a team, teach values, and deal with difficult people issues.

The next level in most organizations is the midlevel manager function, which involves programs aimed at broadening finance, human resources, IT, manufacturing, and other functional leaders. We then

Figure 14-5. Identifiable Teachable Moments

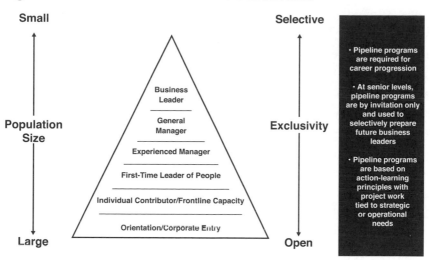

Source: Tichy, Pucik, and Barnett, 1992.

move to the broader leadership population, which in large organizations requires a second-level action learning program below the strategic one described above. Rather than focus on strategic global issues, this program focuses on broadening the leaders to work cross-functionally. The teams are typically made up of multifunctional members who work on organizational improvement projects such as getting manufacturing to cooperate better with engineering or improving the relation between marketing and sales. The skills here are more along the lines of organization development skills than global strategic skills.

Conclusion

The demands on global organizations are going to get tougher and tougher. For Google, Facebook, or older line companies such as Microsoft, Infosys, Lenovo, and the GEs of the world to compete, they must look at tomorrow's leadership pipeline. The leadership pipeline is not limited to the middle and top of the organization but also runs from individual contributors to the next CEO. The more the frontline employees are using their brains to come up with new products and services—which is the case at Google, Amazon, and Best Buy—the more important it becomes to have a frontline-to-CEO leadership development pipeline. This requires the CEO and top management team, with involvement and support from the Board of Directors, to own the process as both social architects and leader-teachers using action learning platforms. Once a CEO grasps the 1 [leadership development] + 1 [task force output] = 4 formula, with twice the return on both, the battle is won. In my experience, the CEO then becomes available for teaching, which in turn sheds a light on the whole organization, and leaders at all levels then become leader-teachers.

Further Reading

Kane, Donald, Noel Tichy, and Eugene Andrews. 1987, November. "Organizational Effectiveness Whitepaper: A Leadership Development Framework." Unpublished.

Tichy, Noel. 1983. *Managing Strategic Change: Technical, Political and Cultural Dynamics.* New York: John Wiley & Sons.

Tichy, Noel. 2003. "The Death and Rebirth of Organizational Development," chapter 10 in *Organization 21C.* Englewood Cliffs, NJ: Financial Times Prentice Hall, 2003.

Tichy, Noel, and Warren Bennis. 2007. *Judgment: How Winning Leaders Make Great Calls.* New York: Penguin Group, 2007.

Tichy, Noel, with Warren Bennis. 2007, October. "Making Judgment Calls." *Harvard Business Review.* Available at http://www.noeltichy.com/pdfs/HBR.pdf.

Tichy, Noel, with Nancy Cardwell. 2002. *The Cycle of Leadership: How Great Leaders Teach Their Companies to Win.* New York: HarperCollins, 2002.

Tichy, Noel, with Eli Cohen. 1997. *The Leadership Engine: How Winning Companies Create Leaders at All Levels.* New York: HarperCollins, 1997.

Tichy, Noel, with Mary Anne Devanna. 1986. *The Transformational Leader.* New York: John Wiley & Sons.

Tichy, Noel, with Andy McGill. 2003. *The University of Michigan Business School's Guide to the Ethical Challenge: How to Lead with Unyielding Integrity*. San Francisco: Jossey-Bass.

Tichy, Noel, with Vladimir Pucik and Carole Barnett, eds. 1992. *Globalizing Management: Creating and Leading the Competitive Organization*. New York: John Wiley & Sons.

Tichy, Noel, with Stratford Sherman. 1993, January. *Control Your Destiny or Someone Else Will: How Jack Welch is Making General Electric the World's Most Competitive Company*. New York: Doubleday/Currency.

Welch, Jack, with John A. Byrne. 2001. *Jack: Straight from the Gut*. New York: Warner Books.

About the Author

Noel M. Tichy is a professor of management and organizations at the Ross School of Business at the University of Michigan, where he is the director of the Global Business Partnership, which for more than a decade ran the Global Leadership Program, a consortium of 36 companies around the world that partnered to develop senior executives and conduct action research on globalization. In 2003, he launched the Global Corporate Citizenship Initiative in partnership with General Electric, Procter & Gamble, and 3M to create a national model for partnership opportunities between business and civil society. To encourage leadership development, he has partnered with a variety of medical systems, the Boys & Girls Clubs of America, and two charter schools in Texas. He also conducts a leadership judgment executive workshop at the University of Michigan. In the mid-1980s, he was head of GE's Leadership Center, the fabled Crotonville, where he led the company's transformation to action learning. Before joining the University of Michigan faculty, he served for nine years on the Columbia University Business School faculty. He is the author of numerous books and articles. His most recent book, with Warren Bennis, is *Judgment: How Winning*

Leaders Make Great Calls (Penguin Group, 2007). He has also co-authored a number of other books, including *Michigan Business School's Guide to The Ethical Challenge: How to Lead with Unyielding Integrity* (with Andrew McGill; Jossey-Bass, 2003); and *The Cycle of Leadership: How Great Leaders Teach Their Companies to Win* (with Nancy Cardwell; HarperCollins, 2002). He has long been regarded as a staple of management literacy, as noted by his rating as one of the top 10 management gurus by *Business Week*.

Leadership as a Competitive Advantage: The Evolution of GE's Growth Values

Jayne Johnson

We all know the importance of aligning our strategic goals for learning and development with those of the organization. Sounds simple enough, right? In practice, however, it can be a challenge. In this chapter, I will share with you the process we follow at General Electric to ensure our company-wide talent management strategy is in lockstep with our learning and development goals.

GE's talent management strategy has four main components: *attract* the best talent, *develop* strong leaders with deep industry and business knowledge, *manage* expectations for success and accountability of their actions, and *retain* the leaders who are the future to GE's continued growth and success. A comprehensive learning and development strategy crosses all four components.

I had the good fortune of working at GE for more than 26 years, the last six of which were at Crotonville, GE's corporate university. There, I was responsible for the overall strategy of GE's cornerstone leadership curriculum, serving GE's top-performing leaders from entry level through early executive. In addition, I managed Crotonville's

Customer Education Team, providing strategic consultative services and training to GE's customers. As a member of Crotonville's executive team, I knew our number one priority was to develop world-class global leaders for GE.

Knowing my main objective, the first thing I needed to do was define "world-class global leadership" in the eyes of my key stakeholders, Jeff Immelt, chairman and CEO of GE, and his senior leadership team. I will share with you an example of how that was accomplished, but first, let me jump ahead and explain what to do with that agreed-upon definition or desired end state once you have it. Then I'll come back and fill in the steps as to how we got there.

If you're a learning professional and someone handed you a list of attributes or characteristics that your stakeholders considered important for effective leadership at your company, you might think you're home free. However, the next step is unfortunately the one that is often overlooked, and without it no learning strategy can be successful. That step is to translate those attributes into behavioral terms. What would it *look* or *sound* like if your leaders displayed these specific behaviors? Let's pick a simple example. If your leadership team thinks "good communication" is an important characteristic for successful leadership, you need to gain agreement on what "good communication" looks like. Does it mean having leaders who can be effective coaches for their direct reports, or leaders who can develop and present a strategic point of view at an executive board meeting? These two potential "definitions" are quite different, and it's important that you gain agreement with your stakeholders on this next level of detail before proceeding further.

Your next step is to frame the skill level needed for your different audiences. For example, the expectations of a "good communicator" for a new manager of individual contributors are probably significantly different than for a leader of a business or function. The new manager has to be proficient enough to perform certain tasks himself or herself, such as creating a vision and communicating that vision to the team, while a leader of a business has to create the vision for the organization AND teach his or her managers how to do the same for their respective teams. The senior leader has to know not only how to "do" but also how to "teach." So the level of sophistication is quite different, not only in terms of scale but also in terms of ability.

Once you have the skills and skill levels defined and agreed upon by your key stakeholders, then it's simply a matter of creating learning experiences to deliver on those expectations. Because this chapter is not a lesson in instructional design principles, I won't go into details; I'll assume you know how to do this already or have a resource to help you with that. What I'd like to share now is an example of this process unfolding at GE. I will share with you the steps we took over the past five years or so to align the strategic goals of learning and development with the evolution of GE's Growth Values.

The Leaders Success Project

I need to go back to 2001 to set the context for this example. That was when Jeff Immelt became chairman and CEO for GE. Shortly after his appointment, he commissioned a project to identify what made some GE leaders succeed while others failed and the associated implications for our leadership development strategy. This project was known as the Leaders Success Project. Once completed, the results became our road map for designing and developing powerful learning opportunities for GE leaders at Crotonville.

The Leaders Success Project started with interviews with 140 senior leaders in the company, or approximately 20 percent of the population. We asked each a series of questions with the purpose of identifying the foundational experiences and skills supporting their success. Each person was also assessed against leadership competencies by his or her direct manager and human resources leader. The results of those interviews and assessments enabled us to construct a career profile for each person. We identified success factors and career derailers. From the pool of 140 leaders, we were able to identify common themes such as how many GE senior leaders

- had graduate degrees
- "grew up" in finance

- graduated from one of GE's entry-level programs (two-year management training program with different tracks for finance, HR, information technology, operations, commercial, and engineering)
- worked outside their home country
- spoke multiple languages.

We also determined the average number of cross-business and cross-functional roles completed by each leader and the average number of years it took for them to reach significant levels of responsibility within the company, like running a business unit.

These common experiences led us to the development of a list of success factors that contributed to the achievements of many GE leaders over the past 100 years, seen in figure 15-1. Some of these factors we consider to be fundamental, and others are key differentiators. The fundamentals are thought of as an "entry ticket." Without it, you won't get far in the leadership ranks. *Integrity* is at the top of that list. At GE, everyone knows "one strike and you're out"—no exceptions. Similarly, you have to be *intelligent,* have strong *business acumen,* and know how to *get things done.* GE is a results-driven company, and we move fast. We expect the same of our leaders. Another foundational expectation is that our leaders are *change agents.* Not only do they need to know how to implement technical changes but probably more important is the people side of change. How do you get people to buy in and support your change efforts so that the changes are sustained for years to come? At GE, we have a process called the Change Acceleration Process that reinforces just that—it's the people side of change that can make or break a new change initiative. The last fundamental factor we identified was proficiency with Six Sigma. This ensures a process improvement mindset that is efficient and puts the customer first.

In addition to these six common elements essential for success, another set of factors or "differentiators" were prevalent in our most successful leaders and separated them from the pack. The first one was being an effective *problem solver.* We encounter problems every day, and a strong leader is resourceful and creative in generating potential solutions.

Figure 15-1. GE Success Factors . . . 100 Years of Great Leaders

Fundamentals	Differentiators
Integrity	**Problem solver**—trade-offs, resourceful, creative
Execution	**Courageous**—pushes back, takes risks, gutsy
Business acumen	**Motivator**—energizes the team, passionate
Change agent	**Learner**—does not make same mistake twice
Intelligence	**Manages the matrix**—able to sell ideas
Six Sigma	**Effective communicator**—verbal, written, presence
	Tenacity—optimistic, faces reality, committed

Second, a leader needs to be *courageous*. He or she is self-confident in taking risks and pushing back respectfully for something they believe in. How many times have you been in a meeting where someone proposes an idea, and someone else shoots it down within seconds? Too many people simply give up at that point and accept criticism without attempting to propose a counterargument or lead a healthy debate regarding their position. If you believe in your idea, then you owe it to yourself to stand up for the idea and push back, but always doing so in a respectful manner. The third differentiator we found among our most effective leaders was being a strong *motivator*. They were passionate and able to channel that passion into motivating their team. Next, they were *life-long learners*. These are the people always looking to learn from their experiences, requesting feedback, and acting on that feedback. Many people do the first part, the asking for feedback. But only the successful few follow through to change their behavior or approach based on the feedback received. Those are the leaders to watch and learn from. *Managing the matrix* was the next differentiator. Being able to get people to help you or believe in your idea when they don't work directly for you requires the ability to influence without positional power. These leaders know who their key stakeholders are and develop a strategy to get them on board early in the process. The next factor, being a *strong communicator*, should come as no surprise. In fact, this could be considered a precursor to many of these other attributes. How can you be a strong motivator if you don't have the communication skills to articulate the vision, and how can you manage the matrix if you don't know how to sell your ideas, which is all about communication? Last, a strong leader needs *tenacity*. He or she needs to be realistic and optimistic simultaneously. Nobody wants to work for a leader who goes around in rose-colored glasses, painting an unrealistic picture. We need to be realistic, but to do that, we need to know the enemy we're fighting. And it helps if we think we have a chance to win so we don't give up. Tenacious leaders stay committed and maintain a positive outlook toward what they believe in.

From this list of fundamentals and key differentiators was born the most valuable outcome from the Leaders Success Project—the leadership framework known as GE's Growth Values (see figure 15-2). These values represent the behaviors Jeff wants in his leadership team, and they are the ones we believe will help GE reach our aggressive growth targets.

There are five GE growth values. First, leaders need to have an *external focus*, defining success in market and industry terms. Second, GE

Figure 15-2. GE's Growth Values

External Focus	• Defines success through the customer's eyes • In tune with industry dynamics; sees around corners
Clear Thinker	• Seeks simple solutions to complex problems; decisive • Focus; communicates clear and consistent priorities
Imagination	• Generates new and creative ideas; open to change • Resourceful; displays courage and tenacity
Inclusiveness	• Teamwork; respects others' ideas and contributions • Creates excitement and drives engagement
Expertise	• Domain depth; credibility built from experience • Continuously develops self; loves learning

Always With Unyielding Integrity

growth leaders need to be *clear thinkers* with the ability to simplify strategy into specific actions and to make tough decisions quickly and efficiently. Next, it's important to have *imagination* and the courage to take risks on people and ideas. The fourth growth value is *inclusiveness*, having the ability to connect with your team and build loyalty so you get the best effort from everyone. The fifth and last growth value is *expertise*. Expertise is all about using depth as a source of confidence to drive change in a specific function or domain.

Jeff had his top 600 leaders assessed in the growth values to establish a baseline of where we stood as an organization. Each leader was rated red, yellow, or green for each trait, and everyone needed at least one red so we could identify our weak links. It turned out that inclusiveness and imagination rated the lowest across the board. These results then became our road map for everything we did at Crotonville. Not only did we develop curricula for the specifics around these skills, but we also integrated growth values into every leadership course. All our leaders were motivated to participate in these programs because they knew learning and demonstrating the values was a critical criteria for success and it was being modeled from the top of the organization.

I hope this example has helped to put in context the importance of aligning your learning and development strategy with that of the organization and offering a suggestion for how you could introduce a similar process in your own organization. GE understands the importance of leadership development, as do many companies these days. As learning professionals, it's our responsibility to ensure we integrate the key priorities of the organization into everything we do every day. That's how we add value and earn respect for the function of learning and development in today's business world.

About the Author

Jayne Johnson joined Deloitte Services LP in October 2010 as chief learning officer, Leadership Development & Succession. In this new role, she oversees customized learning at the firm's new Deloitte University (DU) for high-potential partners and principals. Prior to Deloitte, Jayne spent 26 years at GE, the last six of which were at GE's John F. Welch Centre, also known as Crotonville. During her tenure at Crotonville, she was responsible for the overall strategy of GE's comprehensive cornerstone leadership curriculum, serving GE's top-performing leaders from entry level through early executive. In addition, Jayne managed Crotonville's Customer Education Team, providing strategic consultative services and training to GE's customers.

Jayne began her career at GE on the Information Management Leadership Program (IMLP), one of the company's renowned entry-level leadership programs. She transitioned into L&D within her first 10 years and held various leadership roles over the years. Today, she combines her passion for life-long learning with her technology background to help leaders reach the next level of their professional development capabilities. Her expertise includes leadership development, executive assessments and coaching, employer of choice initiatives, and change management.

Developing the Appreciated Leader: Leader Development at a Teaching Hospital

Rebecca Phillips, with Jane Binger

Leadership in an academic healthcare setting often originates from deep expertise in a discipline such as radiology or cardiology. Discipline leaders are recognized for deserved reputations in research, clinical care, and education. They are, by academic standards, successful. This success is based on the quality and efficient delivery of systems of care, basic and clinical research, and services to develop the next generation of healthcare leaders in research, clinical care, and education. Yet, individually, these leaders wish for better preparation for their business and organizational responsibilities. Consequently, the learning and development function is responsible for supporting both business and academic success.

L&D's expected role is to deliver training on requirements, initiatives, and a standard portfolio for workforce and leader development, as seen in business and industry. Leaders are responsible for focusing the staff and material resources. L&D teaches the organizational effectiveness and business systems in which leaders are expected to excel (allowing leaders to practice mastery of those systems so that employees will adopt them); and L&D teaches the leader behaviors or competencies (which constitute the leader profile) necessary to get work done through people. In an academic healthcare setting, the outcomes of learning's role in leader development are defined as leader readiness and leader performance, demonstrated by improved systems thinking, adoption of best practices, translation of research to the bedside, and the best possible patient outcome and experience.

Knowledge of people and business systems results in an expanded view of the leaders' full scope of responsibility, answering the question "What does it mean to be a manager and leader in this organization?" As in other fields, a strategic view is essential, and the effort to bridge the department and institutional strategies is an L&D role in leader development.

A variety of methods makes this happen. The advantages of classroom learning focusing on an institutional issue or a simulation to run a hospital creates a network and helps participants see how what they do affects others. More important, the classroom opportunity to meet the executives of business functions helps managers understand how they each contribute to fulfilling the mission and influencing effectiveness and compliance. Putting a "face to the necessary bureaucracy" enables large organizations to thrive while enhancing improvement efforts. Online training allows for greater consistency and can incorporate "live" messages from executives. It can also provide easy access to references when needed, draw on infrequently used systems, and refresh the training when many changes occur simultaneously. Online and in-person training occurs 24/7 in the hospital, with sessions conducted where people work.

Specific behaviors and competencies are required as leaders prepare strategic plans and then run the operations to achieve their strategic objectives and goals. To delineate leader profiles and expectations, many healthcare organizations draw on the leadership literature and the services of professional organizations such as Jim Kouzes and Barry Posner's Leadership Challenge (www.leadershipchallenge.com) and the National Center for Healthcare Leadership. Effective executive development in healthcare reinforces alignment in these ways:

- Expectations and profiles are decided in cooperation with organization executives. The definitions and examples should be theirs.

- The resulting profile is measured against benchmarks in an assessment center.

- The results from the assessment center are then used to establish individual strategic goals aligned with the institution's strategic direction, with clear expectations. Individual learning plans are created with an internal coach, who helps the participants and their line managers identify and prepare resources for learning.

- L&D offers training on competencies, during which participants specify the strategic initiative to which they will apply the new competency, aligned with their individual goals. This strategic area is meant to be worked on during a specified time period.

- Following training on each competency, participants in learning and goal-setting events are supported by coaching, directed readings, and discussion sessions.

- Participants speak with others about how they are applying the competencies to accomplish individual goals.

- Business results are also tied to the competencies in business unit reports when executives comment on strategic and operational progress. Organization leaders are involved in development.

L&D is a common thread throughout talent management; for example, workforce and succession planning use the same competency sets; orientation functions as part of onboarding, teaching goal setting; tuition reimbursement is done as part of rewards, providing a system for individual learning plans; and education research and measurement are tied to outcomes and best education practices. Engagement comes from executive sponsorship and from applying competencies to achieve organizational and individual goals. Development is provided for leaders at various stages through these programs:

- Leadership development for all includes formal open enrollment programs and performance feedback.

- Emerging talent includes individual and organizational needs and interests and diversity strategy.

- The Accelerated Development Program for high-potential staff is characterized by customized experience and learning, high resources, and high touch.

- Succession development addresses both short and long horizons for specific positions.

The Honest Broker

L&D is the honest broker that convenes the organization's leaders to ensure that the full system is functioning together. The launch of a new electronic medical record system is an example of this broker role. An incorrectly implemented EMR system could result in patient risk or even harm. A professional literature review found that the implementation of EMRs in some organizations resulted in more errors in patient care. This was deemed to be a "never event." The launch of the new EMR was preceded by a review of clinical work flows, so high-quality improvement tools and skills were needed. Staff members learned both new processes and a new computer system.

The executive team recognized that leaders were critical to the success of the EMR's implementation, so the L&D professionals convened leaders from IT, HR, facilities, and various clinical areas for ongoing change management and problem escalation/resolution. A simulation or "playground" of the new system was made available so people could learn while "working," see common errors, and make mistakes without causing harm. The L&D function demonstrated the integrated use of classroom and e-learning. The evaluation results showed comparable levels of learning and application on the job—all reinforced by leader messages, walk-arounds, and Q&A sessions and other in-person interactions. Patient errors did not increase during the implementation of the EMR, and targeted efficiencies were achieved.

The best evidence of L&D's successful role in leader development can be found in responses from the participants themselves. Here's a sample response. The learning experience "pointed out to me the importance of shared vision by leaders and the hospital. This has made me share more of myself, my vision, and model this more for others. It has given me a much larger view of my potential impact at this institution over my formal title and job responsibilities. Now I participate more in the leadership of this organization."

The Same but Different

There are similarities in leader development between academic and nonacademic environments. And there are differences. Two features distinguish L&D in an academic healthcare setting. One is its unique role in providing deep education and training expertise to faculty and other professionals whose jobs include training others. The other is the use of evidence-based education practices.

Academic hospitals are critical for the preparation of healthcare professionals nationally and globally. Accrediting bodies specify competencies across trainee programs. Yet there often isn't time in the healthcare curriculum for the acquisition of the expertise to develop and deliver these trainee programs. At one academic hospital, L&D staff members partnered with the directors of fellowships to create the core curriculum required of all fellows. The benefits derived from this partnership included the elimination of redundant work; the opportunity for physicians to serve as subject matter experts and to have more time in their practices and to develop specialized training; the chance to have content delivered in many ways to suit learners and their schedules; and the spreading of the best content and practices across the institution.

How does L&D integrate with the clinical, research, and education missions of an academic health center?

- We help define, obtain, and use knowledge of the institution's priorities.
- For large system rollouts, we make systems linkages explicit and support leader advocacy of the system. These rollouts require

many training rooms and computers, so we partner with these facilities. Small and medium-sized enterprises know the content but not always how to share it, so we train them in facilitation skills or co-facilitate.

■ We identify skills and train based on them; these skills include change management, coaching, feedback, employee engagement, computer applications, work-flow process, technology changes, and improvement science.

■ We demonstrate proof of training's impact using evidence in the form of evaluations of long-term patient outcomes and the impact on learners. We look at how much success is attributed to training and how confident the leaders are in their ability to perform.

■ We recognize and address areas of leader discomfort—potential errors, patient risk, changing people's job roles (for example, for EMR work flow), and job descriptions (performance management system).

■ We offer more than training events. We use many types of media to reinforce learning and create opportunities for peer learning.

Evidence-based education practices are fundamental for academic healthcare L&D. During the performance management and fellowship core curriculum implementation, all facilitators received their evaluation feedback. If target evaluation scores were not achieved, then the facilitators and designers made changes to improve the results vis-à-vis learner satisfaction, the impact on patient outcome, new learning, application on the job, and the overall value to the organization.

These evaluation results and educator performance improvements were published and reported to the hospital's executives and board members. Learner performance was further supported by providing online job aids and walk-in sessions based on evaluation results. Managers, applying new coaching and feedback skills, reported accelerated application of the new performance system and greater readiness for performance discussions.

At our teaching hospital, the learning and development function is essential because we create opportunity for individuals to set strategic and personal goals, we explicitly target learning to these goals and objectives, and we provide rigorous evidence of the impact on learners, on the organization, and on the results achieved with our young patients.

About the Author

Rebecca Phillips, PhD, is vice president for education and learning and an associate professor at Cincinnati Children's Hospital and Medical Center. Previously, she was training director and deputy director, human resources, at Los Alamos National Laboratory and director of organizational research and associate director of the Center for Knowledge Management at Motorola University. Her research, teaching, publications, and international presentations include establishing organizational learning services, systems, and business plans (alignment with organization objectives); evidence-based adult education outcomes and financial assessment; applying improvement science to learning and development; educator and faculty development; and mentoring. She received a doctorate in curriculum and instruction and adult education (learning and development) from the University of New Mexico.

Jane Binger, executive director of leadership development and education at Lucile Packard Children's Hospital at Stanford University Medical Center, also contributed to this chapter. She received her BS in nursing, MA in Education–Administration and Policy Analysis, and EdD in Education–Administration and Policy Analysis from Stanford University.

Section VIII

■ ■ ■

Pulling It All Together

17

Integrated Talent Management

Dave Ulrich

Most can recite and readily recognize the changing landscape of business. Globalization makes the world both more uniform with global standards and more diverse with sensitivity to local customs and cultural differences. Technology makes the world more connected, smaller, and faster, as technology has moved from 1.0 with a focus on efficiency, to 2.0 with a focus on information, to 3.0 with a focus on relationships. Demographics have shaped workforce expectations as employees have learned to work across generational and global boundaries (see chapter 2 by Peter Cappelli on changing business conditions).

All these unending changes and challenges to business have moved talent to the forefront of business success (ASTD, 2009). Competitors quickly match price, product, and operations, but they have a more difficult time matching talent. Talent differentiates, drives productivity, determines customer service, and increases intangible shareholder value. Talent matters. Talent is too important to be left to uncoordinated events.

But as talent has become ubiquitous and important, it has also become more difficult to operationalize. Too often the term "talent" has taken on the black-box characteristics of concepts such as "quality," "strategy," and "vision," as if it was a Rorschach test for business leaders where talent can mean whatever a business leader or writer wants it to mean. In this chapter, I try to synthesize and simplify the talent field into 12 principles. Each principle captures not only what has happened but also what should happen in developing talent. Each principle also has leadership implications for offering a more integrated approach to talent management.

Principle 1: Define the Talent Targets and Tailor Talent Initiatives

Principle 1 is to define the talent targets and to tailor talent initiatives. I was working in a company where the external board challenged the management team to invest more rigorously in "talent." The pleas were both demanding and emotional, with claims that talent was the key to the future and that management should spend more time on talent. But when the executives worked to respond to these expectations, they were not sure where to start. It was helpful to them to begin by specifying five talent targets—shown in the first column of table 17-1—each of which required a different talent investment.

As explained in table 17-1, each of these talent targets has different challenges, key issues, and required initiatives. Thus CEO succession entails personalized assessments and plans to prepare backups for key leadership positions. The senior leadership cohort suggests improving the senior leadership group by building competency models and development experiences. Developing high-potential employees (generally about 10 to 15 percent of total population) starts with early identification of these future leaders, then cleverly increasing their development opportunities to prepare them for their future. For all employees, you need to ensure that the employee has the skills to do the work, the commitment to work hard, and an ability to find meaning from doing the work. And creating a talent-oriented organizational culture suggests that teams work together to meld individual talents into teamwork and that an organization develops a positive reputation for talent.

As each of these five areas is worked on individually and collectively, an overall definition of talent can be crafted: Talent is a systematic process (not an event) to secure general and targeted individual competencies (what people know, do, and value) and organization capabilities (not just a person, but also a culture) that create sustainable value for multiple stakeholders (employees, customers, and investors).

> Leadership implication: Be very clear about whom you mean by talent. Who are the targets of your talent investments?

Principle 2: Talent Matters Inside a Company— and Outside

Principle 2 is that talent matters inside a company—and outside. Few would argue with the premise that organizations with better talent will be more successful, as defined by increased productivity (Dorgan and Dowdy, 2002), the ability to execute a strategy (Hrebiniak, 2005; Bossidy, Charan, and Buck, 2002), the extent to which there are backups in place for key positions (Rothwell, 2005), and employee engagement scores (Buckingham and Coffman, 1999).

In addition, talent may also be linked to external stakeholder outcomes. If a company has better talent, then we are likely to see increased customer, investor, and community value. A talent–customer value proposition exists where organizations with employees who have a more positive attitude will likely have customers who match that attitude (Schneider and Bowen, 1995; Ulrich et al., 1991; Schneider et al., 2009). Increasingly, there is a shared understanding that intangibles represent up to 50 percent of the market value of a publicly traded company. These intangibles represent the confidence that investors have in a firm's ability to predictably deliver future earnings (Ulrich and Smallwood, 2003) and are rooted in how investors perceive the quality of the organization's employees. Companies work hard within their communities to build a reputation, which both enables firms to attract better employees and helps employees feel better about their work (Dowling, 2002).

> Leadership implication: Leaders should spend 20 to 25 percent of their time identifying, upgrading, and improving talent.

Table 17-1. Talent Targets

Talent Target	Key Challenge	Key Issues	Example Initiatives
CEO and senior executives	Managing succession	• How do the senior leaders make sure that they have viable successors in place? • How does a succession process work so that backups are prepared to move into key roles?	• Backup plans • Succession planning process
Senior leaders	Building a leadership cohort	• How do senior leaders (approximately the square root of the total number of employees) develop the competencies to run the company in the future? • How do we place skilled leaders in key positions?	• Leadership competency models • Leadership academy and training • Matching person and position
High-potential employees	Identifying and developing future leaders	• How can high-potential employees be identified (ambition, agility, ability, and achievement)? • How can high-potential employees have individual development plans that prepare them for the future?	• Identification of those with high potential • Personalized development plans

All employees	Upgrading talent processes throughout the organization	• How can all employees develop the competencies to do their current and future work? • How can employees increase their commitment? • How can employees find more contribution or meaning from their work?	• Integrated human resources solutions in recruiting, training, compensation, and performance management • Improving commitment or engagement scores • Helping build meaning at work
Organizational culture	Investing in a talent culture	• How can leaders shape a culture that encourages talent? • How can individual abilities be forged into organization capabilities?	• Organization audits • Development of high-performing teams

Source: Compiled by the author.

Principle 3: Talent Requires Individual Ability— and Teamwork

Principle 3 is that talent requires individual ability—and teamwork. Talent matters, but teamwork matters more. At the Academy Awards, about 15 percent of the time, the best picture of the year also has the best actor or actress. In professional basketball, soccer, and hockey, about 15 percent of the time, the team with the top scorer has won the overall championship. Like movies and sports, business today requires teamwork. In a world where knowledge (as measured by information on the Internet) doubles every four years, where the pace of change has increasingly increased, and where global complexity changes the rules of competition, no isolated individual has the ability to respond. To have sustainable organizations in a world of change and complexity, individual abilities must be combined into organization capabilities. Talent requires teamwork.

> Leadership implication: Leaders should not only attend to defining and developing skills of individuals but also to auditing and improving teamwork and organizational culture.

Principle 4: Talent Should Align Competencies With Strategy Inside—and Stakeholders Outside

Principle 4 is that talent should align competencies with strategy inside—and stakeholders outside. Most talent work begins with competencies. Competencies represent the knowledge, skills, and abilities of employees (White, 1959; McClelland, 1973, 1976; Boyatzis, 1992). Historically, competencies have been identified by comparing low- and high-performing employees vis-à-vis critical incidents and determining a set of behaviors that distinguish the two (Flanagan, 1954; Andersson and Nilsson, 1964). More recently, competencies have been aligned with the strategy of a business (Lado and Wright, 1992; Burgoyne, 1992; Byham and Moyer, 1996). Competencies have more impact when they help a business deliver its goals.

Going forward, competencies inside a company may be aligned with the expectations of customers, suppliers, communities, and investors outside the company. The "right" competencies are those that align external expectations and internal actions (Ulrich and Smallwood, 2007). These customer-centric competencies then become standards for leaders and employees throughout the company. When competency models start with future customer expectations, they direct employee attention to what they should know and do. We often test competency models by showing the television commercials of a company. These externally focused statements define what the organization wants to be known for by external stakeholders. Then we match those expectations with the competencies identified in the competency model. In most of our work to date, the overlap between external expectations and internal competency models needs improvement.

> Leadership implication: Make sure that the leadership and other competency models tie to external customer expectations.

Principle 5: Talent Requires Assessment, Both Inside and Outside

Principle 5 is that talent requires assessment, both inside and outside. Based on defined competencies, standards may be established whereby employees may be assessed on how well they perform. In recent years, most individual talent assessments have had some form of a balanced scorecard (Kaplan and Norton, 1996, 2001, 2006). For individuals, this logic has led to evaluating individuals on both results and behaviors (Slater, 1998; Welch and Welch, 2005). Talented employees deliver results that may be related to financial, customer, and organization outcomes. In addition, talented employees behave the right way based on how well they demonstrate the defined competencies. These competencies may be assessed by the employee, subordinates, peers, and supervisors through 360-degree feedback (Tornow and London, 1998; Lombardo and Eichinger, 2004). See the summary of assessment and appraisal by Ed Lawler in chapter 8.

However, to provide a holistic view, employees may also be evaluated by those outside the organization—suppliers, customers, investors, community leaders, and other external stakeholders. This shifts the 360-degree feedback to 720-degree feedback (360 x 2 = 720). And 720-degree feedback initiatives assess internal employee actions relative to external customer expectations.

> Leadership implication: Make sure that the performance management and assessment tools take into account external expectations and observations and focus on the future, not just the past.

Principle 6: Talent Comes From Thoughtful Investment That Encourages Collaboration

Principle 6 is that talent comes from thoughtful investment that encourages collaboration. The billions of dollars spent on upgrading talent may be seen as investments in building future talent. I suggest six types of investments that upgrade global talent, with thoughts on how to look forward to more innovative talent management:

- *Buying*—recruiting, sourcing, securing new talent into the organization (Smart and Street, 2008; see chapter 4 by John Sullivan). Increasingly involve customers or suppliers to source, interview, and orient new employees.

- *Building*—helping people grow through training, on the job, or life experiences (Landale, 1999; Harrison, 2005). Create executive exchanges where employees take assignments in customer or supplier organizations, involve customers or investors in design, and delivery of development programs. In chapter 14, Noel Tichy thoroughly reviews GE's Crotonville development process.

- *Borrowing*—bringing knowledge into the organization through outsourcing, advisers, or partners (Reuer, 2004). Source knowledge from contractors or others outside the organization; create web-based social networks to find ways of doing work.

- *Bounding*—promoting the right people into key jobs (Rothwell, 2005). Consider customer and investor expectations when doing succession planning.

- *Bouncing*—removing poor performers from their jobs and/or the organization (De Meuse and Marks, 2003). Use customer criteria as part of the downsizing process, and outplace employees into supplier or customer networks.

- *Binding*—retaining top talent (Kaye and Jordan-Evans, 2008; see chapter 12). Be willing to rehire talented employees who have left; use employee referral programs to not only identify and attract future employees but also as a way to retain the best employees.

The assessment of and investment in talent needs to be done systematically to reflect the changing nature of the business. Top companies make sure that talent plans are as flexible as their strategic plans (see chapter 9 by Annmarie Neal and Robert Kovach, and chapter 11 by Rob Reindl).

> Leadership implication: Create aligned, integrated, and innovative approaches to upgrading talent that include job experience, development experiences, and life experiences.

Principle 7: Talent Needs to Be Mindful of, and Gain the Benefits From, Individual Differences (Diversity)—and Build Unity

Principle 7 is that talent needs to be mindful of, and gain the benefits from, individual differences (diversity)—and build unity. Diversity awareness enables organizations to encourage variety in thinking and acting along a number of dimensions—race, age (generational shifts), gender, national culture, psychological orientation, career drivers, and global perspective. Managing diversity has social implications as societies assimilate people with different backgrounds, political ramifications as legislation attempts to serve multiple stakeholders, and economic consequences as organizations increase innovation and creativity by bringing together people with different backgrounds (Thomas, 2005). Internal diversity matters more as organizations operate in increasingly complex social and economic settings.

Although many organizations have implemented diversity or inclusion initiatives that foster respect for individual differences, I would also suggest that diversity without unity creates chaos. Simply respecting, responding to, or encouraging people who are different to come together will not result in better organizational performance if those people do not have a common goal and ability to work together. When they do so, societies, political systems, and organizations move forward. Organizations that maximize diversity without unity will devolve into disorder with respect for differences being an excuse for disconnected actions. Organizations that foster true diversity also have explicit unity. Unity needs to be centered on working for common goals that generally begin with customer orientation.

> Leadership implication: Make sure that there
> are clear, shared, and active principles that
> govern employee behaviors; they maximize
> diversity around everything else.

Principle 8: Talent Should Focus on the A Players— but Also Pay Attention to B Players

Principle 8 is that talent should focus on the A players—but also pay attention to B players. Top performers produce a disproportionate amount of results (Smart, 2005). More recently, top performers have been labeled

"A" players (versus B or C players), and leaders have been encouraged to match A players to A positions, which are those wealth-creating roles where top individuals can have maximum impact (Huselid, Beatty, and Becker, 2005). Top performers in key roles will generally produce stronger results. There is a myth that A players may be portable and that their skills may be sourced and shifted across organizational boundaries. Recently, scholars have been finding that it is even more important to retain top players than to attract them (Groysberg and Abrahams, 2010; Groysberg and Lee, 2009; Fernandez-Araoz, Groysberg, and Nohria, 2009).

However, B players are also important. "B" players are more likely to stay with the company (versus A players who are more mobile); there are more B players; B players are the heart and soul of a company and carry the institutional memory of the company (DeLong and Vijayaraghavan, 2003). When leaders find ways to engage B players without having to make them into A players, the organization builds a more comprehensive commitment throughout the organization.

> Leadership implication: Acknowledge the A players, but pay attention to the B players.

Principle 9: Talent Requires Not Only Competence and Commitment but Also Contribution

Principle 9 is that talent requires not only competence and commitment but also contribution. A simple formula for talent has been competence x commitment (Ulrich, 1998). Competence means that individuals have the knowledge, skills, and values required for today's and tomorrow's jobs. One company clarified competence as *right skills, right place, right job*. Competence clearly matters, because incompetence leads to poor decision making. But without commitment, competence is discounted. Highly competent employees who are not committed are smart, but they don't work very hard. Committed or engaged employees work hard, put in their time, and do what they are asked to do. In the last decade, commitment and competence have been the bailiwicks for talent.

However, the members of the next generation of employees may be competent (able to do the work) and committed (willing to do the work), but unless they are making a real contribution through the work (finding meaning and purpose in their work), then their interest in what they are doing will diminish and their productivity will wane. Contribution occurs when employees feel that their personal needs are being met through their participation in their organization. Organizations are the universal setting in today's world where individuals find abundance in their lives through their work, and they want this investment of their time to be meaningful. Simply stated, competence deals with the head (being able), commitment with the hands and feet (being there), and contribution with the heart (simply being). An emerging talent formula might be: competence x commitment x contribution = talent (Ulrich and Ulrich, 2010).

> Leadership implication: Become a meaning
> maker as you couple the motions and actions
> of leadership with emotion and passion.

Principle 10: Technology Facilitates Talent Management Processes—and Connection Among People

Principle 10 is that technology facilitates talent management processes— and connection among people. Technology has changed the way talent work is organized and delivered through information sharing, improved processes, redefinitions of work, and social networks. Technology enables individuals to source and share information from people who are not personally accessible. The Internet's initial use was to be a more efficient and accessible encyclopedia where people could gain and share information.

Technology also improves talent processes (Kavanagh and Thite, 2008). Technology-enabled staffing includes employee databases such as Monster.com and web-based succession planning systems. Technology facilitates training and development by defining and assessing competencies and by using video and other web-based training programs. Reward systems are also technology-enhanced to more efficiently administer the process of setting goals, holding people accountable for goals, and allocating rewards. Technology handles the administrative requirements of talent management. Technology also redefines work boundaries.

Through technology, knowledge becomes an asset that does not need to be owned to be accessed. With technology, employees may work in a company without having a physical presence there. With technology, organizations can now accomplish work using individuals who have no formal or long-term relationship with the organization. Technology also creates social networks that enable people to connect with each other not just to share information but also to become part of a personal and professional community (Safko and Brake, 2009). As technology evolves from wireless networks to satellite transmissions to cloud computing to artificial neural networks, people become connected across time and space. These swarms of talented individuals focus attention, make decisions, and sustain social support.

> Leadership implication: Become comfortable
> with technology-enabled talent management.

Principle 11: Talent Activities Need to Be Measured—as Do Talent Outcomes

Principle 11 is that talent activities need to be measured—as do talent outcomes. Talent measures traditionally track activities related to talent—how many were hired, how they were hired, where they were hired from, what percent of leaders received 40 hours of training, how participants felt about training, or what percent were promoted based on succession plans (Fitz-enz, 2001, 2009). These activity-based talent metrics help assess the processes related to talent, but they do not fully capture the outcomes of talent initiatives. Talent outcomes would be the response to the question "If we have better talent, what happens?" Some of these talent outcomes could be related to individuals (retention, productivity, preparation for promotion, or engagement). And some of them could be tracked in relation to organizational capabilities (speed of response, innovation, customer service) (Ulrich, 1990, 1997; Ulrich and Smallwood, 2004). The new return-on-investment of human resources (or talent) is return-on-*intangibles*—where investor confidence in future business success is measured by intangible shareholder value (Ulrich and Smallwood, 2006).

> Leadership implication: Create a rigorous talent assessment process that tracks not only activities but also outcomes.

Principle 12: Talent Efforts Need to Be Owned by Line Managers—and Created by Human Resources and Learning and Development Professionals

Principle 12 is that talent efforts need to be owned by line managers—and created by human resources and learning and development profession-als. Four groups of stakeholders might be involved with building talent (Ulrich et al., 2009):

- Line managers own talent initiatives and ensure that they align to business goals (see chapter 3 by Teresa Roche, which explains the importance of CEO involvement in talent management).

- Human resources and learning and development leaders create talent initiatives (see the introduction by Oakes and Galagan).

- Consultants and advisers offer frameworks and insights from others and point out lessons learned.

- External customers and investors guide the relevance of talent work.

Line managers are ultimately accountable for ensuring that the organization has the right talent and right organization in place to deliver on expectations to customers, shareholders, and communities. The term "line manager" refers to leaders at all levels of the organization. Members of the Board of Directors should be informed about the rationale for and outcomes of talent investments. Line managers in the C-suite (governing or executive committee) should be informed advisers for talent efforts. Line managers throughout the organization should also be aware of talent, how it will affect their ability to reach their goals, and what their role will be in helping it move forward.

Talent depends on the quality of HR (including learning and development) professionals and their relationships with line managers (Ulrich et al., 2008). If they cannot respond to the increased expectations raised by talent demands, they will quickly lose credibility and be relegated to second-tier status. Three targets are important among HR professionals: chief HR officer (CHRO), learning and development professionals, and HR professionals. The CHRO needs to be the talent sponsor by allocating money and time to the talent effort. The CHRO should initiate, take the lead in the design, and monitor the talent plan, ensuring that robust measurements are in place to credibly and accurately monitor progress. The learning and development professionals offer expertise and insights into all types of development activities (see chapter 16 by Rebecca Phillips, with Jane Binger). A talent transformation may be sponsored by the CHRO, but it must be enacted and lived by learning and development professionals throughout the organization. HR and learning and development professionals who embrace talent initiatives recognize that their personal success is linked to the success of the HR transformation. HR professionals become architects who build frameworks and offer ideas to line managers.

Consultants or advisers bring insights and ideas into the talent arena. A colleague who has deep expertise in merger and acquisition integration recently shared that he had been retained to help a client manage a merger integration. But the client, in an effort to cut costs, opted to not use these services and worked to integrate the merger without outside counsel. Six months later, they had not realized the synergies they promised the investment community when they made the merger, key employees had left, the combined company strategy was haphazard, and leaders were questioning if they had made the right choice in the merger. No one can guarantee that our colleague could have averted these problems, but he had experience in dozens of companies that had faced and overcome these and other problems. Judicious and targeted use of outside consultants as partners may advance talent investments. Consultants may add value by bringing in experiences from other companies, by previewing and averting common challenges, by not being beholden to a political system that might limit creative problem solving, and by being independent contributors to the talent management process.

The customer and investor perspectives are critical to informed talent decisions. When there is a line of sight from external expectations to internal talent actions, those actions will more likely be sustained.

> Leadership implication: Make sure that your approach to talent includes an integrated solution with experts from line departments, HR, and learning and development.

Summing Up

To make assessing your own talent management efforts easier, these 12 principles and the auditing questions that go with them are summarized in table 17-2.

Talent matters. No one disputes this in both good and bad economic conditions. But when we can turn the complex and almost unmanageable array of talent ideas into basic principles, leaders can begin to improve their talent efforts.

Table 17-2. Integrated Talent Assessment

Talent Principles	Diagnostic Questions
1. Define talent targets	• How well do we delineate the different talent targets? • How well do we tailor our talent investments to the specific needs of each target group?

2.	Talent matters inside a company—and outside	• How well do we link talent to the stakeholders both inside and outside the company (employees, organization, customer, investor/owners, community)? • How much time do our senior leaders spend on improving talent?
3.	Talent requires individual ability—and teamwork	• How well do we manage teamwork within our organization? • How well do we focus on key organization capabilities that define our culture?
4.	Talent should align competencies with strategy inside—and stakeholders outside	• How well do we link competencies to business success? • How often do we link internal competencies to external expectations from customers, investors, and communities? • How well do our internal competencies match external expectations?
5.	Talent requires assessment both inside—and outside	• How well do our assessments connect employee behaviors with external expectations? • How well do we use multiple assessment methods (psychological tests, assessment centers, etc.)? • How well do we tie assessments to rewards and other consequences?
6.	Talent comes from thoughtful investment that encourages collaboration	• How well do we bring new people into the organization? • How well do we develop talent with job assignments? • How innovative are our training experiences? • How well do we invest in talent through promotion systems? • How well do we integrate all the talent investment activities into a cohesive approach to talent?

7. Talent needs to be mindful of individual differences—and unity	• How well do we pay attention to diversity of age, gender, race, global background, education background, ethnicity, and work style? • How well do we emphasize the areas in which we must have unity in order to succeed?
8. Talent matches players to positions	• How well do we differentiate players (A, B, C)? • How well do we differentiate key positions? • How well do we match players to positions? • How well do we attend to the B players?
9. Talent requires competence and commitment—and contribution	• How well do we work to define and increase employee engagement? • How well do we gauge and increase employees' sense of contribution? • How well do we help employees find meaning at work?
10. Technology facilitates talent management—and connects people	• How well have we used technology to make our talent management processes more efficient? • How well do we use technology to connect people to each other?
11. Talent activities need to be measured—and outcomes	• How well do we measure the activities related to talent? • How well do we measure the outcomes of talent activities?
12. Talent is owned by line managers . . . and architected with human resources and learning and development professionals	• How well do we hold line managers accountable for talent management efforts? • How well do we build a partnership among line managers, human resources professionals, and learning and development professionals to upgrade talent?

Source: Compiled by the author.

References

Andersson, B.-E., and S.-G. Nilsson. 1964. "Studies in the Reliability and Validity of the Critical Incident Technique." *Journal of Applied Psychology* 48: 398–403.

ASTD. 2009. *2009 State of the Industry Report.* Alexandria, VA: ASTD Press. Available at www.astd.org.

Bossidy, Larry, Ram Charan, and Charles Buck. 2002. *Execution: The Discipline of Getting Things Done.* New York: Crown Business.

Boyatzis, Richard. 1992. *The Competent Manager: A Model for Effective Performance.* San Francisco: Wiley.

Buckingham, Marcus, and Curt Coffman. 1999. *First, Break All the Rules: What the World's Great Companies Do Differently.* New York: Simon & Schuster.

Burgoyne, John. 1992. "The Competence Movement: Issues, Stakeholders and Prospects." *Personnel Review,* 22, no. 6: 6–13.

Byham, William, and Reed Moyer. 1996. *Using Competencies to Build a Successful Organization.* Minneapolis: Development Dimensions.

DeLong, Tom, and V. Vijayaraghavan. 2003. "Let's Hear It for B players." *Harvard Business Review,* June, 96–102.

De Meuse, Kenneth P., and Mitchell Lee Marks, eds. 2003. *Resizing the Organization: Managing Layoffs, Divestitures, and Closings.* San Francisco: Pfeiffer.

Dorgan, Stephen, and John Dowdy. 2002. "How Good Management Raises Productivity." *McKinsey Quarterly,* November.

Dowling, Graham. 2002. *Creating Corporate Reputations.* Oxford: Oxford University Press.

Fernandez-Araoz, Claudio, Boris Groysberg, and Nitin Nohria. 2009. "The Definitive Guide to Recruiting in Good Times and Bad." *Harvard Business Review,* May, 74–84.

Fitz-enz, Jac. 2001. *How to Measure Human Resource Management,* 3rd ed. New York: McGraw-Hill.

———. 2009. *The ROI of Human Capital: Measuring the Economic Value of Employee Performance.* New York: AMACOM.

Flanagan, J. 1954. "The Critical Incident Technique." *Psychological Bulletin* 51, no. 4: 327–58.

Groysberg, Boris, and Robin Abrahams. 2010. "Managing Yourself: Five Ways to Bungle a Job Change." *Harvard Business Review*, January–February.

Groysberg, Boris, and Linda-Eling Lee. 2009. "Hiring Stars and Their Colleagues: Exploration and Exploitation in Professional Service Firms." *Organization Science*, July–August, 740–58.

Harrison, Rosemary. 2005. *Learning and Development*. London: CIPD Publishing.

Hrebiniak, Lawrence. 2005 *Making Strategy Work: Leading Effective Execution and Change*. Philadelphia: Wharton School Publishing.

Huselid, Mark, Richard Beatty, and Brian Becker. 2005. "'A Players' or 'A Positions'? The Strategic Logic of Workforce Management." *Harvard Business Review*, December.

Kaplan, Robert, and David Norton. 1996. *The Balanced Scorecard: Translating Strategy into Action*. Boston: Harvard Business Press.

———. 2001. "Transforming the Balanced Scorecard from Performance Management to Strategic Management." *Accounting Horizons* 15.

———. 2006. *Alignment: Using the Balanced Scorecard to Create Corporate Synergies*. Boston: Harvard Business Press.

Kavanagh, Michael, and Mohan Thite. 2008. *Human Resource Information Systems: Applications and Future Directions*. Thousand Oaks, CA: SAGE.

Kaye, Beverly, and Sharon Jordan-Evans. 2008. *Love 'Em or Lose 'Em: Getting Good People to Stay*, 4th ed. San Francisco: Berrett-Kohler.

Lado, Boyd, and Patrick Wright. 1992. "A Competency-Based Model of Sustainable Competitive Advantage: Toward a Conceptual Integration." *Journal of Management* 18: 77–91.

Landale, Anthony. 1999. *Gower Handbook of Training and Development*. Farnham, UK: Gower Publishing.

Lombardo, Michael M., and Robert W. Eichinger. 2004. *FYI: For Your Improvement*. Minneapolis: Lominger.

McClelland, David. 1973. "Testing for Competence Rather Than Intelligence." *American Psychologist* 28, no. 1: 1–14.

———. 1976. *A Guide to Job Competency Assessment*. Boston: McBer.

Reuer, Jeffrey, ed. 2004. *Strategic Alliances*. New York: Oxford University Press.

Rothwell, William. 2005. *Effective Succession Planning: Ensuring Leadership Continuity and Building Talent from Within.* New York: AMACOM.

Safko, Lon, and David Brake. 2009. *The Social Media Bible: Tactics, Tools, and Strategies for Business Success.* New York: Wiley.

Schneider, Benjamin, and David Bowen. 1995. *Winning the Service Game.* Boston: Harvard Business Press.

Schneider, Benjamin, William Macey, Karen Barbera, and Nigel Martin. 2009. "Driving Customer Satisfaction and Financial Success through Employee Engagement." *People and Strategy* 32: 24–27.

Slater, Robert. 1998. *Jack Welch and the G.E. Way: Management Insights and Secrets of the Legendary CEO.* New York: McGraw-Hill.

Smart, Bradford. 2005. *Topgrading: How Leading Companies Win by Hiring, Coaching, and Keeping the Best People.* Englewood Cliffs, NJ: Prentice Hall.

Smart, Geoff, and Randy Street. 2008. *Who: The A Method for Hiring.* New York: Ballantine.

Thomas, Roosevelt. 2005. *Building on the Promise of Diversity: How We Can Move to the Next Level in Our Workplaces, Our Communities, and Our Society.* New York: AMACOM.

Tornow, Walter, and Manuel London. 1998. *Maximizing the Impact of 360-Degree Feedback: A Process for Successful Individual and Organizational Development.* Greensboro: Center for Creative Leadership.

Ulrich, Dave. 1989. Tie the Corporate Knot: Gaining Complete Customer Commitment. *Sloan Management Review,* Summer, 19–28.

———. 1990. *Organization Capability: Competing from the Inside/Out.* New York: Wiley.

———. 1997. *Human Resource Champions: The Next Agenda for Adding Value and Delivering Results.* Boston: Harvard Business Press.

———. 1998. "Intellectual Capital = Competence * Commitment." *Sloan Management Review,* Winter, 15–26.

Ulrich, Dave, Justin Allen, Wayne Brockbank, Jon Younger, and Mark Nyman. 2009. *HR Transformation: Building Human Resources from the Outside/In.* New York: McGraw-Hill.

Ulrich, Dave, Wayne Brockbank, Dani Johnson, and Kurt Sandholtz. 2008. *HR Competencies: Mastery at the Intersection of People and Business.* Washington: Society of Human Resource Management.

Ulrich, Dave, Richard Halbrook, Dave Meder, and Mark Stuchlik. 1991. "Employee and Customer Attachment: Synergies for Competitive Advantage." *Human Resource Planning* 14, no. 2: 89–102.

Ulrich, Dave, and Norm Smallwood. 2003. *Why the Bottom Line Isn't: How to Build Value through People and Organization.* Boston: Harvard Business Press.

———. 2004. "Capitalizing on Capabilities." *Harvard Business Review,* June.

———. 2006. "HR's New ROI: Return on Intangibles." *Human Resource Management* 44: 137–42.

———. 2007. *Leadership Brand: Developing Customer-Focused Leaders to Drive Performance and Build Lasting Value.* Boston: Harvard Business Press.

Ulrich, Dave, and Wendy Ulrich. 2010. *The Why of Work: How Great Leaders Build Abundant Organizations to Deliver Value to Employees, Customers, Investors, and Communities.* New York: McGraw-Hill.

Welch, Jack, and Suzy Welch. 2005. *Winning.* New York: HarperBusiness.

White, R. 1959. "Motivation Reconsidered: The Concept of Competence." *Psychological Review* 66, no. 5: 297–333.

About the Author

Dave Ulrich is as a professor of business at the University of Michigan and a partner in the RBL Group, a consulting firm focused on helping organizations and leaders deliver value. He studies how organizations build capabilities of speed, learning, collaboration, accountability, talent, and leadership by leveraging human resources. He has helped generate award-winning databases that assess alignment between strategics, human resource practices, and human resources competencies. He has published more than 100 articles and book chapters and 22 books. He has won numerous lifetime achievement awards and has consulted with more than half of the Fortune 200 companies.

18

All Together Now: The Practical Realities of Talent Management Integration

Kevin D. Wilde

"I ntegrated talent management" is one of the top buzz phrases in the learning and development industry. The main idea is that by aligning the various disciplines and data streams of talent efforts, we can create higher value and more work that will make an impact. Visualize the various boxes of HR specialties all lined up neatly in columns and rows, with lines and arrows linking everything together, like schoolchildren holding hands while crossing the road.

In my own organization, we have seen the significance of talent integration. For example, a common, simple, yet powerful set of leadership expectations is embedded in recruiting and selection routines, which are brought to life in career development and learning systems, rewarded and reinforced with performance coaching and incentives, and relied upon for succession and talent forecasting initiatives. HR performs from a common playbook and is guided by a mutual scorecard. It's not perfect, and it needs constant attention to keep the integration glue holding, but the reward of work that has more of an impact is apparent.

Unfortunately, integration isn't easy and can quickly degrade over time. The reality is that knitting talented beings together is hard work, because there are as many forces pulling us apart as pushing us together. Figure 18-1 illustrates the magnitude of the challenge.

Why Apart? It's the People

Classic organization design practices cause work to be broken down into subunits for efficient focus and resource optimization. And it usually works quite well:

- The good people in compensation create programs to deliver cost-effective and competitive pay practices.

- The skilled professionals in recruiting bring in the most qualified new employees as quickly as possible.

- The pros in learning and development produce online and classroom material for all those well-paid and well-placed employees.

- HR generalists cast a narrow field of view when offering HR services to a slice of the organization, hoping for a little more help and a little less distraction from compensation, recruiting, and training.

Figure 18-1. Integration Is a Challenge for All Organizations

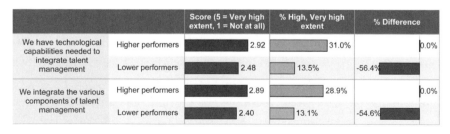

		Score (5 = Very high extent, 1 = Not at all)	% High, Very high extent	% Difference
We have technological capabilities needed to integrate talent management	Higher performers	2.92	31.0%	0.0%
	Lower performers	2.48	13.5%	-56.4%
We integrate the various components of talent management	Higher performers	2.89	28.9%	0.0%
	Lower performers	2.40	13.1%	-54.6%

Source: Data collected by the Institute for Corporate Productivity and ASTD.

- The strategies and objectives are isolated from each other.

- The cycle of new practices and change initiatives springs forth mostly independently.

- Rewards and resources go to subsets, rarely the whole.

Blending and integrating is an unnatural act. Each HR tribe attracts a certain type of talent:

- Like numbers and analytics? *Compensation clan.*

- Like being a teacher? *Learning gang.*

- Get charged up finding new friends? *Recruiting squad.*

- Rather take action than do too much analyzing? *Generalist posse.*

HR tribes generate their own mini-cultures and jargon. They see their spots in the organization and how to add value differently. Most important, they individually strive to be shining examples of business partners at the big table and not those poor HR souls dismissed by line clients to the kid's picnic bench in the back.

Why Apart? It's the System

The information age of HR ushered in automation to more efficiently manage the transactions of each subgroup (each one state of the art with a different software vendor):

- compensation systems to process payroll and incentives

- recruiting systems to sort résumés and track candidates

- learning management systems to document competencies and course completions.

Over time, attempts have been made to link these systems. The best systems providers are promoting integrated, full-suite talent management systems. The evolution is promising, but the conversion process usually means that someone gives up their favorite functionality for the greater (promised) good.

How Together?

There are barriers aplenty to integration, but there is hope as well. It takes extra effort and the kind of intelligent, willful change management effort that we advise line organizations to apply. In my experience, I have seen a few common enablers that pull the practices and systems of talent management together:

- common planning
- clear accountabilities and measures
- competent processes
- collaborative values.

Let's explore each of these practices in more detail.

Common Planning

Think *short-term* thematic and *long-term* strategic. The author and consultant Patrick Lencioni presents the useful idea of a thematic goal as a way to pull multiple departments together. Thus, I've seen the power of crafting a talent management thematic goal by posing the question "If we don't get anything else done in the next six months together, we must do . . . ?" Then, by getting specific multiple-unit efforts behind the common thematic goal, a road map is created to achieve the collective mission. Once the short-term thematic goal is reached, the common planning cycle is repeated, and short-term success builds momentum.

Long-term strategic goals pull together the various HR teams to sketch out a road map for three to five years. A good offsite retreat or a burst of half-day sessions of the key players can create the long-range common plan as well as provide time to build cohesion. As rework, consider a small cross-sectional team to draw out a holistic representation of how the various HR units are currently integrated and where the key value-creating processes and practices cut across organization boundaries. When the full group gathers, here are useful questions to think through together aloud:

- What are the most critical business needs, strategies, and capability needs in the next three to five years that call for a common HR approach? This topic is better tackled in a top-down approach versus a roll-up of the disparate subfunction goals and views.

■ Where can the various components of HR be better linked together to coordinate the achievement of these long-range objectives?

■ How do we see our collective strengths, weaknesses, opportunities, and threats in our integrated approach? Which of these factors is most important to address, and what actions should we consider?

■ Where could we leverage our resources together? How can we best evolve our information systems to enable the common mission?

■ In the future, how can we better coordinate our individual strategic plans?

Clear Accountabilities and Measures

Integration means great teamwork and, much as in the sports world, winning teams perform well because they have clearly understood and coordinated individual contributions. It is all too common to find promising HR initiatives unwind due to the simple lack of dedicated time to establish and revisit role expectations. An integrated talent management thematic, once established, should be followed by answering the question "Who is going to do what, by when, to make this happen?" Agreed-upon roles and responsibilities can grow fuzzy or impractical as the constant march of change has an impact on the organization. Revisiting and renegotiating sessions are ways to keep everyone accountable and in sync.

Closely related to defining accountabilities is clarifying the guideposts of common work progress measurements. As systems improve, useful data scorecards can be crafted to keep everyone tracking the same way. The danger here is to either rely on each specialty's metrics or chase reported numbers that fall short of generating insight or action. Here again, upfront discussions on scorecard items that reflect agreed-upon indicators of progress and desired outcomes are better than just an aggregation of HR department reports. This is where the new generation of integrated talent management software holds the most promise in providing a common, linked database offering a single view of the numbers and useful, enterprise- or initiative-wide scorecards.

Competent Processes

Smart, integrated talent management software installations take the right amount of time to map out the current and optimal way a process occurs and then configure the information system to effectively enable the complete practice, not just any one subunit. Getting different HR departments together in a room to create a mutual view of how real work happens is always educational and sometimes transformational. But don't let the software impose new practices that are too aggressive. I've never seen an organization overcome poor managerial talent management habits by imposing a sophisticated out-of-the-box software package.

Another dimension of competent processes to address when integrating is the need to set some informal rules of the road for tackling work together. An underserved or forgotten aspect of collaborative effort is taking time to overtly agree how decisions and trade-offs will be made as work progresses. Decide where empowerment rests in a particular department and where advanced consulting and input gathering across boundaries is called for. Establish where communication and information flow need to be strengthened for big projects and sticky work handoffs. Certainly, new technologies can keep everyone in the loop better. I've seen the quality of cross-team decision making and communication improve by simply opening up HR department meetings to a broader audience, even establishing rotated representation spots to formalize the connection.

Collaborative Values

Let's be candid here: There can be peer jealousies and functional infighting across HR departments. Integrating the "hardware" of talent management calls for investing in the "software" of mutual trust and collaboration. Devoting time to bring different groups together to renew healthy relationships is as smart an investment as any new software package or redrawing the HR organization chart. As mentioned above, we might all live under the big HR tent, but we tend to camp out with our subspecialties with our own secret handshakes and rituals. This is just normal human nature, but it's still the biggest long-term threat to integration.

All the traditional tools of trust building and team cohesion apply here. Useful routines include dedicated meetings and meals together, where getting to know you better is the main course. I know time is short and it's a hard commitment to maintain, considering the rush of business today. Think of it this way: All pro sports teams begin with time for training before the season begins. World-class orchestras and performing arts companies devote countless hours to practicing together to find the optimal blend of extraordinary individual talent and group unity. Can we in HR skip that, jump onstage together, and expect flawless performances? Not likely.

Finally, seemingly rock-solid interpersonal trust can crack under reward and recognition routines that elevate individual unit accomplishment above common achievement. Adding new ways to reward "together" and decreasing individual incentives can be the sustaining element for all the common goal setting, coordinated roles, supportive systems, and routines. Set up mutual bonus pools or incentives based on overarching organizational or broad HR initiative success. Strengthen community celebrations and increase your recognition of common achievements (and heartfelt support when we fall short together). Moreover, the greatest enabler is the most senior HR leader who really values collaboration and teamwork across the various HR units. Public team leadership and private coaching solidify the value of collaboration.

In conclusion, integrated talent management is really managing naturally divergent HR teams more than installing a shiny, new mega-software system. The reality is that dynamic forces pull us apart more than they push us together, and in so many ways—how we organize to approach our work and how we overspecialize when growing our HR talent. But there is nonetheless hope, and I see four main ways to pursue better-integrated talent management in HR:

- To begin, initiate new planning routines where common thematic objectives are set in functionwide strategy development sessions.

- Next, ensure solid coordination efforts across the HR organization, with clearly understood and supported roles to integrate work.

- Back up the goals and roles with better-coordinated processes, including enhanced communication, inclusive decision making, and problem solving that brings operational excellence for the greater good.

- Finally, invest in the magic ingredient of all high-performing teams: the value and willingness to work together despite any shortcomings in the legacy organization design and traditions.

About the Author

 **Kevin D. Wilde** is vice president and chief learning officer at General Mills, Inc., where he is responsible for worldwide talent management, executive development, and the Leadership Institute. In 2007, *Chief Learning Officer* magazine selected him as CLO of the year. Before joining General Mills, he spent 17 years at General Electric in a variety of human resources positions in the healthcare and capital divisions, as well as corporate assignments at GE's renowned leadership center, Crotonville. He is a columnist for *Talent Management* magazine and serves on the editorial boards of a number of professional journals. His work has been published in more than a dozen books, including the chapter "The General Mills & Pillsbury Merger" in *Coaching for Leadership: The Practice of Leadership Coaching from the World's Greatest Coaches* (2nd ed., Pfeiffer, 2005), and the *Pfeiffer Annual on Leadership Development* (Pfeiffer, various years). He received a bachelor's degree in marketing and education from the University of Wisconsin–Stout and a master's degree in administrative leadership and adult education from the University of Wisconsin–Milwaukee.

Additional Research From ASTD and i4cp

Introduction: Too Many Soloists, Not Enough Music

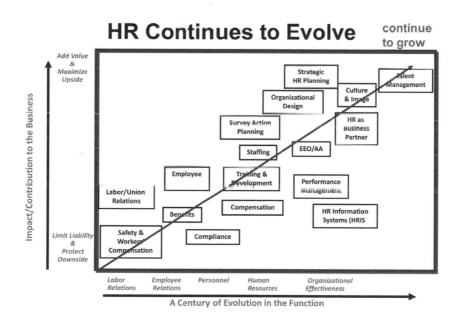

Section I: Overview of Integrated Talent Management

Integrated Talent Management Model

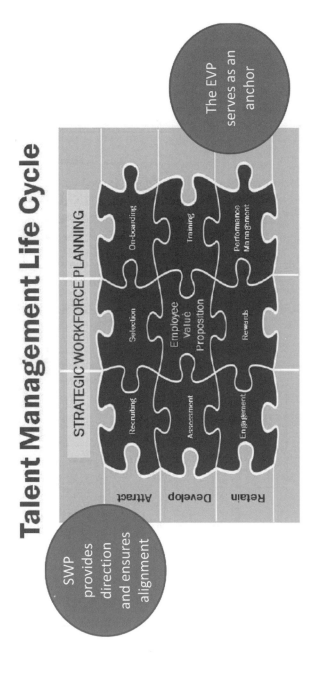

Talent Management Life Cycle

Higher Performing Organizations (HPO) Are More Effective At Managing Talent

Overall, to what extent is your organization managing talent effectively?

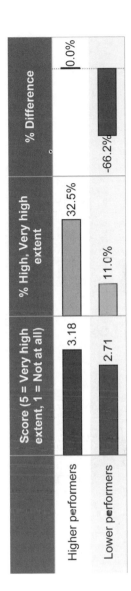

What Do High Performance Organizations Include in Talent Management?

		Score (5 = Very high extent, 1 = Not at all)	% High, Very high extent	% Difference
Performance management	Higher performers	3.83	70.2%	0.0%
	Lower performers	3.64	57.4%	-18.3%
Learning/training	Higher performers	3.88	70.2%	0.0%
	Lower performers	3.48	51.5%	-26.7%
Leadership development	Higher performers	3.80	64.8%	0.0%
	Lower performers	3.39	52.5%	-19.0%
High-potential employee development	Higher performers	3.58	58.7%	0.0%
	Lower performers	3.18	46.5%	-20.8%
Compensation and rewards	Higher performers	3.46	54.1%	0.0%
	Lower performers	3.04	37.0%	-31.6%
Individual professional development	Higher performers	3.47	51.6%	0.0%
	Lower performers	3.03	38.0%	-26.4%
Succession planning	Higher performers	3.32	48.4%	0.0%
	Lower performers	2.96	37.6%	-22.2%
Competency management	Higher performers	3.29	47.5%	0.0%
	Lower performers	2.77	25.3%	-46.9%
Engagement	Higher performers	3.40	47.1%	0.0%
	Lower performers	2.86	32.7%	-30.7%
Recruitment	Higher performers	3.45	46.7%	0.0%
	Lower performers	2.97	38.4%	-17.8%

Section II: Recruiting

Engagement Starts With Recruitment

What do you look for in new recruits?

Organizations with Highly Engaged Employees	Organizations with Disengaged Employees
1. Has passion for work	1. Intelligent
2. Has positive attitudes toward peers and customers	2. Confident in work abilities
3. Has desire to set and achieve goals	3. Has excellent job skills
4. Adaptable	4. Has positive attitudes toward peers and customers
5. Intelligent	5. Emotionally mature
6. Confident in work abilities	6. Has passion for work
7. Has excellent job skills	7. Has desire to set and achieve goals

Most Organizations Rate the Effectiveness of Their Recruitment Efforts to Be About Average

Overall, how would you rate the effectiveness of your organization's recruitment efforts?

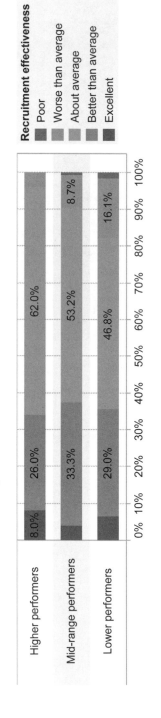

Section III: Compensation and Rewards

Pay for Performance

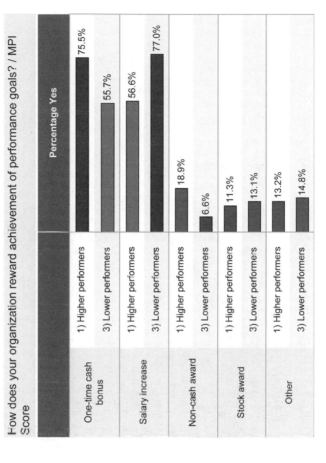

How does your organization reward achievement of performance goals? / MPI Score

	Percentage Yes
One-time cash bonus	
1) Higher performers	75.5%
3) Lower performers	55.7%
Salary increase	
1) Higher performers	56.6%
3) Lower performers	77.0%
Non-cash award	
1) Higher performers	18.9%
3) Lower performers	6.6%
Stock award	
1) Higher performers	11.3%
3) Lower performers	13.1%
Other	
1) Higher performers	13.2%
3) Lower performers	14.8%

To what extent does your organization use the following to measure HR?

Responses of all companies with over 10,000 employees

		Measure	Don't measure and don't care to	Considering / Developing
Payroll or Labor expense as a percentage of total operating cost (e.g. Cost of labor is 40% of total operation expense)	1) Higher Performers	72.4%	6.9%	20.7%
	3) Lower Performers	89.3%	7.1%	3.6%
Ratio of HR to total staff or ratio of employees to HR staff	1) Higher Performers	72.4%	6.9%	20.7%
	3) Lower Performers	81.5%	18.5%	
HR expense, percent of company's operating costs	1) Higher Performers	69.0%	10.3%	20.7%
	3) Lower Performers	71.4%	21.4%	7.1%
HR cost by HR function (staffing, compensation, etc.)	1) Higher Performers	48.3%	20.7%	31.0%
	3) Lower Performers	57.1%	25.0%	17.9%
HR cost by business line	1) Higher Performers	39.3%	39.3%	21.4%
	3) Lower Performers	57.7%	30.8%	11.5%
Other	1) Higher Performers	25.0%	75.0%	
	3) Lower Performers		100.0%	

Comparison of Higher-performing companies and lower-performing companies

Source: i4cp HR Metrics Interactive Data, 2009

Section IV: Performance Management

High-Performance Organizations Understand the Power of Performance Management

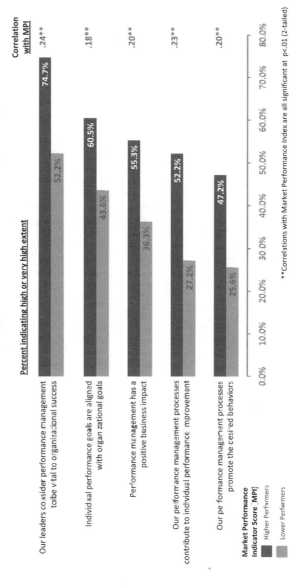

To what extent are the following statements true about your organization?

Percent indicating high or very high extent

Statement	Higher Performers	Lower Performers	Correlation with MPI
Our leaders consider performance management to be vital to organizational success	74.7%	52.2%	.24**
Individual performance goals are aligned with organizational goals	60.5%	43.6%	.18**
Performance management has a positive business impact	55.3%	36.3%	.20**
Our performance management processes contribute to individual performance improvement	52.2%	27.2%	.23**
Our performance management processes promote the desired behaviors	47.2%	25.6%	.20**

Market Performance Indicator Score (MPI)
- Higher Performers
- Lower Performers

0.0% 10.0% 20.0% 30.0% 40.0% 50.0% 60.0% 70.0% 80.0%

**Correlations with Market Performance Index are all significant at p<.01 (2-tailed)

229

Performance Management Results Are Used More Often by High-Performance Organizations

To what extent is your organization's performance management process used for the following?

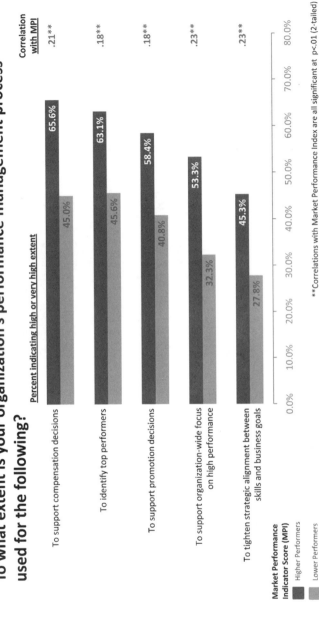

Percent indicating high or very high extent

	Higher Performers	Lower Performers	Correlation with MPI
To support compensation decisions	65.6%	45.0%	.21**
To identify top performers	63.1%	45.6%	.18**
To support promotion decisions	58.4%	40.8%	.18**
To support organization-wide focus on high performance	53.3%	32.3%	.23**
To tighten strategic alignment between skills and business goals	45.3%	27.8%	.23**

Market Performance Indicator Score (MPI)
■ Higher Performers
■ Lower Performers

**Correlations with Market Performance Index are all significant at p<.01 (2-tailed)

Performance Management was found to be the Most Integrated Component of Talent Management

Talent Management Integration Scores *

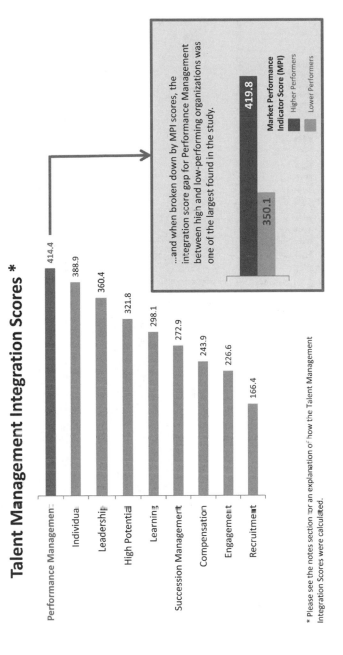

Performance Management — 414.4

Individual — 388.9

Leadership — 360.4

High Potential — 321.8

Learning — 298.1

Succession Management — 272.9

Compensation — 243.9

Engagement — 226.6

Recruitment — 166.4

...and when broken down by MPI scores, the integration score gap for Performance Management between high and low-performing organizations was one of the largest found in the study.

Market Performance Indicator Score (MPI)

419.8 — Higher Performers

350.1 — Lower Performers

* Please see the notes section for an explanation of how the Talent Management Integration Scores were calculated.

The 9 Keys to Performance Mgt.

1. The performance management process includes developmental plans for the next period

2. Training is provided to managers on conducting a performance appraisal meeting

3. The quality of performance appraisals is measured

4. There is a system in place to address and resolve poor performance

5. The performance appraisal includes information other than that based on the judgment of managers

6. The performance management process is consistent across the organization

7. Employees expect feedback on their performance more often than once a year

8. 360° or multirater feedback is used to support the performance management process

9. The performance management process includes an ongoing goal review and feedback from managers

Section V: Succession Management

Companies Tend to Focus Internally When Seeking Talent

To what extent do you seek talent _outside_ the organization for your succession planning pipeline?

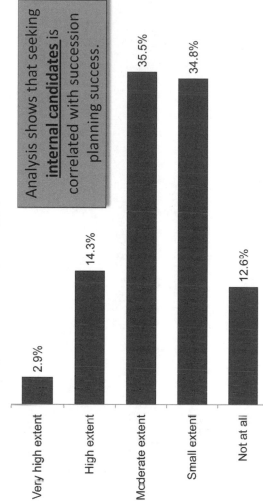

Analysis shows that seeking _internal candidates_ is correlated with succession planning success.

- Very high extent — 2.9%
- High extent — 14.3%
- Moderate extent — 35.5%
- Small extent — 34.8%
- Not at all — 12.6%

Leadership development is integral to succession planning

To what extent does your organization's learning function play the following roles in the succession planning process?

Responses	Percentage Answering High or Very High Extent	Correlation with SPSI	Correlation with MPI
Defining content for leadership development programs	55.6%	.18**	
Delivering training to succession candidates	46.6%	.25**	.16**
Integrating succession planning with other talent management processes	37.0%	.28**	
Management/oversight of succession planning	36.1%	.12*	
Follow-up/evaluation of succession planning efforts	32.1%	.20**	.09*
Identifying candidates for the succession planning process	22.5%	.24**	

* Correlation is significant at $p < .05$ (2-tailed)
** Correlation is significant at $p < .01$ (2-tailed)

The learning function's investments in succession planning pay dividends

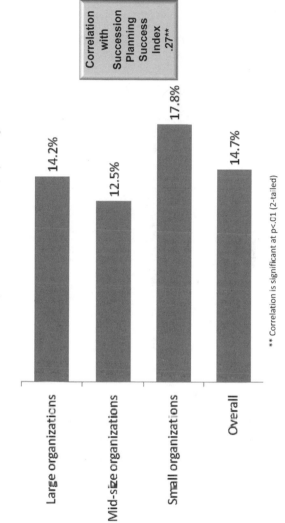

What percentage of your organization's overall learning budget is used to fund development related to succession planning?

Correlation with Succession Planning Success Index .27**

Large organizations — 14.2%

Mid-size organizations — 12.5%

Small organizations — 17.8%

Overall — 14.7%

** Correlation is significant at p<.01 (2-tailed)

The lack of good development plans is, far and away, the most commonly cited barrier to succession plans

To what extent do the following factors pose challenges for your succession planning?
Top ten responses

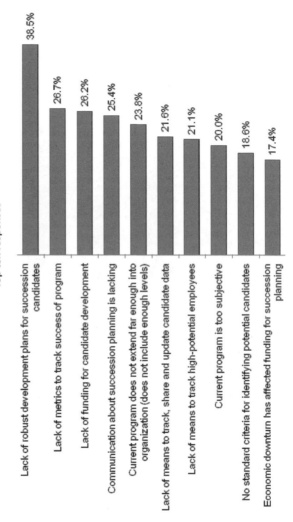

Lack of robust development plans for succession candidates	38.5%
Lack of metrics to track success of program	26.7%
Lack of funding for candidate development	26.2%
Communication about succession planning is lacking	25.4%
Current program does not extend far enough into organization (does not include enough levels)	23.8%
Lack of means to track, share and update candidate data	21.6%
Lack of means to track high-potential employees	21.1%
Current program is too subjective	20.0%
No standard criteria for identifying potential candidates	18.6%
Economic downturn has affected funding for succession planning	17.4%

Percentage answering high or very high extent

Section VI: Engagement and Retention

To what degree does your organization consider the following to be key indicators that employees are engaged in their work? Top ten responses

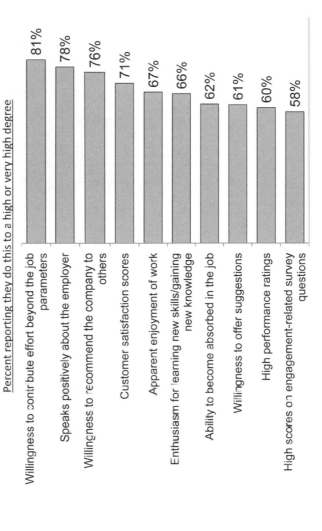

Percent reporting they do this to a high or very high degree

Willingness to contribute effort beyond the job parameters	81%
Speaks positively about the employer	78%
Willingness to recommend the company to others	76%
Customer satisfaction scores	71%
Apparent enjoyment of work	67%
Enthusiasm for learning new skills/gaining new knowledge	66%
Ability to become absorbed in the job	62%
Willingness to offer suggestions	61%
High performance ratings	60%
High scores on engagement-related survey questions	58%

High market performers have more highly engaged employees

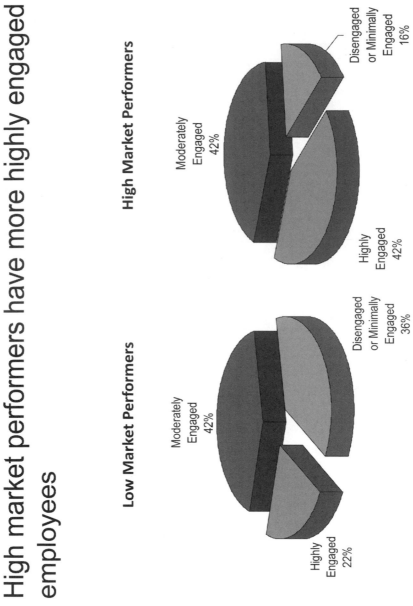

Low Market Performers

Moderately
Engaged
42%

Highly
Engaged
22%

Disengaged
or Minimally
Engaged
36%

High Market Performers

Moderately
Engaged
42%

Highly
Engaged
42%

Disengaged
or Minimally
Engaged
16%

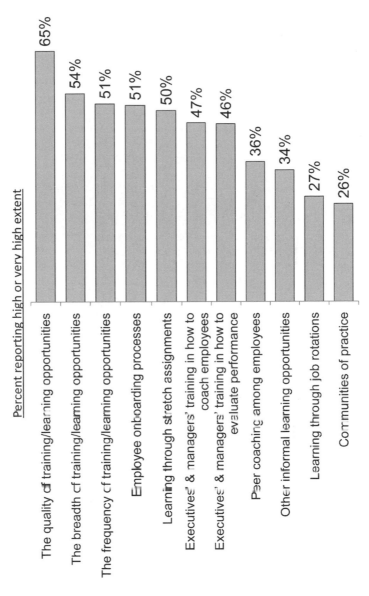

To what extent do the following factors positively influence employee engagement in your organization?

Percent reporting high or very high extent

The quality of training/learning opportunities — 65%
The breadth of training/learning opportunities — 54%
The frequency of training/learning opportunities — 51%
Employee onboarding processes — 51%
Learning through stretch assignments — 50%
Executives' & managers' training in how to coach employees — 47%
Executives' & managers' training in how to evaluate performance — 46%
Peer coaching among employees — 36%
Other informal learning opportunities — 34%
Learning through job rotations — 27%
Communities of practice — 26%

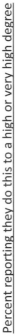

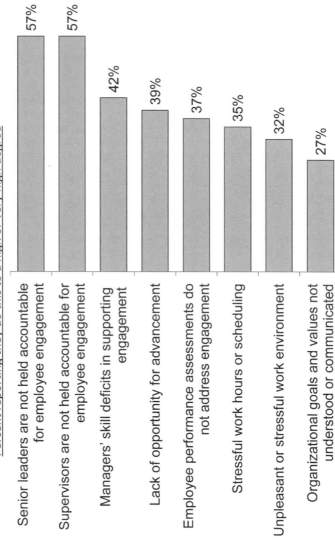

To what degree are these barriers to engagement in your organization? Top eight responses

Percent reporting they do this to a high or very high degree

Barrier	Percent
Senior leaders are not held accountable for employee engagement	57%
Supervisors are not held accountable for employee engagement	57%
Managers' skill deficits in supporting engagement	42%
Lack of opportunity for advancement	39%
Employee performance assessments do not address engagement	37%
Stressful work hours or scheduling	35%
Unpleasant or stressful work environment	32%
Organizational goals and values not understood or communicated	27%

Rate the following factors in terms of their ability to drive employee engagement

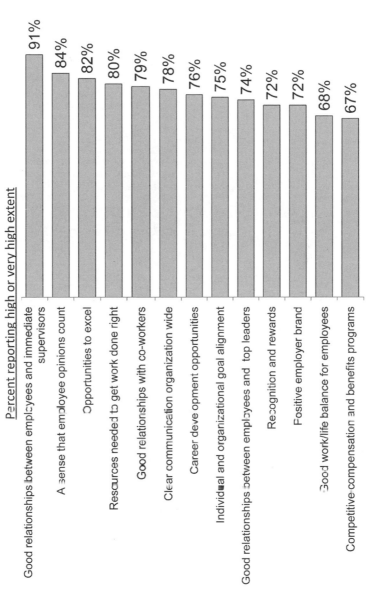

Percent reporting high or very high extent

- Good relationships between employees and immediate supervisors — 91%
- A sense that employee opinions count — 84%
- Opportunities to excel — 82%
- Resources needed to get work done right — 80%
- Good relationships with co-workers — 79%
- Clear communication organization wide — 78%
- Career development opportunities — 76%
- Individual and organizational goal alignment — 75%
- Good relationships between employees and top leaders — 74%
- Recognition and rewards — 72%
- Positive employer brand — 72%
- Good work/life balance for employees — 68%
- Competitive compensation and benefits programs — 67%

Section VII: Leadership Development

Higher performers and those with a higher leadership success score report stronger existing leadership and leadership development programs

To what extent do you agree with the following statements? / Market Performance Index (MPI Score)

		Score (1=Not at all, 5=Very high extent)	% High extent, Very high extent	% Difference
The excellence of my organization's top leadership team (officer level) surpasses most in our industry	Higher performers	3.31	50.0%	0.0%
	Lower performers	2.59	25.0%	-50.0%
My organization emphasizes the continuing development of its current leaders' skills	Higher performers	3.20	44.6%	0.0%
	Lower performers	2.50	27.0%	-39.5%
My organization is strong at developing future leadership talent	Higher performers	2.86	29.5%	0.0%
	Lower performers	2.16	13.2%	-55.1%

Higher performers are more likely to use tools and training to build leadership competencies

To what extent does your organization use each of the following tools and training techniques to build leadership competencies? / MPI Score

Top ten responses by % High extent, Very high extent

		Score (1=Not at all, 5=Very high extent)	% High extent, Very high extent	% Difference
Performance management / development plan	Higher performers	3.11	39.8%	0.0%
	Lower performers	2.74	23.7%	-40.4%
Online or e-learning systems	Higher performers	2.78	29.3%	0.0%
	Lower performers	2.42	22.4%	-23.6%
Internal coaching sessions	Higher performers	2.47	21.5%	0.0%
	Lower performers	2.03	12.2%	-43.5%
360-degree feedback	Higher performers	2.41	19.2%	0.0%
	Lower performers	1.91	10.8%	-43.8%
Corporate university	Higher performers	2.15	18.5%	0.0%
	Lower performers	1.64	12.0%	-35.2%
Mentoring	Higher performers	2.54	15.9%	0.0%
	Lower performers	2.12	9.1%	-42.7%
"Off the shelf" courses from external suppliers	Higher performers	2.33	15.0%	0.0%
	Lower performers	2.12	14.9%	-0.9%
Rotational assignments (short-term, up to six months)	Higher performers	2.15	13.4%	0.0%
	Lower performers	1.68	5.3%	-60.2%
Onboarding (or "reboarding") when a leader transitions to a new assignment	Higher performers	2.09	12.3%	0.0%
	Lower performers	1.70	5.4%	-56.2%
Customized programs from external suppliers	Higher performers	2.08	11.4%	0.0%
	Lower performers	1.88	12.3%	8.2%

Good strategy execution and business knowledge top the list of successful leadership characteristics

Out of all the following leadership competencies, select the six that best characterize the most successful leaders in your organization: / MPI Score

	Higher performers	Lower performers
They execute strategy well	57.0%	50.0%
They know the business well	54.4%	58.1%
They know our customers well	54.4%	47.3%
They create an environment of trust / respect	45.5%	47.3%
They develop strategy well	44.3%	39.2%
They have good communication skills	43.0%	37.8%
They are good decision-makers	43.0%	40.5%
They have strong business ethics	41.8%	43.2%
They build relationships well	40.5%	41.9%
They have high levels of emotional intelligence	24.1%	29.7%
They know how to align the organization well	22.8%	23.0%
They have good change management skills	22.8%	16.2%
They know how to motivate	19.0%	20.3%
They manage talent well	17.7%	23.0%
Other	6.9%	9.5%

Higher performers are more likely to measure leadership development effectiveness

To what extent does your organization use each of the following methods to assess leadership development effectiveness? / MPI Score

		Score (1=Not at all, 5=Very high extent)	% High extent, Very high extent	% Difference
Individuals' performance	Higher performers	3.72	65.8%	0.0%
	Lower performers	3.23	52.7%	-19.9%
Overall business results	Higher performers	3.55	58.4%	0.0%
	Lower performers	3.17	48.6%	-16.8%
Participant reaction to development programs	Higher performers	2.57	26.7%	0.0%
	Lower performers	1.89	7.0%	-73.6%
Readiness for promotion	Higher performers	2.54	23.0%	0.0%
	Lower performers	2.16	14.5%	-36.9%
Time to competency	Higher performers	2.07	13.2%	0.0%
	Lower performers	1.76	5.9%	-55.6%
Before- and after-training/development tests	Higher performers	1.91	10.7%	0.0%
	Lower performers	1.51	2.8%	-74.0%

Section VIII: Putting It All Together: A Truly Integrated Talent Management Organization

An effectively Integrated Talent Management process is positively correlated with Market Performance

Please state the extent to which you agree with the following statements:

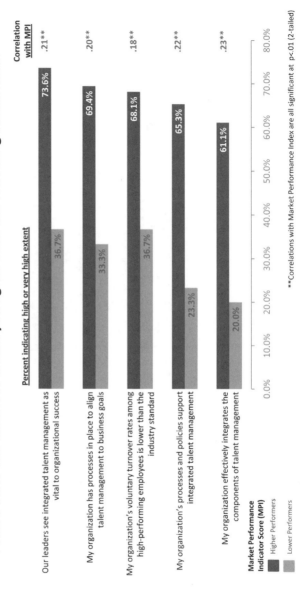

Percent indicating high or very high extent

Correlation with MPI

Our leaders see integrated talent management as vital to organizational success — Higher Performers: 73.6%, Lower Performers: 36.7%, .21**

My organization has processes in place to align talent management to business goals — Higher Performers: 69.4%, Lower Performers: 33.3%, .20**

My organization's voluntary turnover rates among high-performing employees is lower than the industry standard — Higher Performers: 68.1%, Lower Performers: 36.7%, .18**

My organization's processes and policies support integrated talent management — Higher Performers: 65.3%, Lower Performers: 23.3%, .22**

My organization effectively integrates the components of talent management — Higher Performers: 61.1%, Lower Performers: 20.0%, .23**

Market Performance Indicator Score (MPI)
- Higher Performers
- Lower Performers

**Correlations with Market Performance Index are all significant at p<.01 (2-tailed)

How Do High Performance Organizations Measure TM Effectiveness? (Hint: Think Business Metrics)

		Score (5 = Very high extent, 1 = Not at all)	% High, Very high extent	% Difference
Customer satisfaction rates	Higher performers	3.21	50.5%	0.0%
	Lower performers	2.43	29.5%	-41.6%
Market share	Higher performers	2.85	43.0%	0.0%
	Lower performers	1.90	14.6%	-66.1%
Revenue	Higher performers	2.85	40.6%	0.0%
	Lower performers	2.08	20.6%	-49.2%
Performance appraisal ratings	Higher performers	2.99	40.6%	0.0%
	Lower performers	2.79	33.3%	-17.8%
Training and development effectiveness	Higher performers	2.98	38.3%	0.0%
	Lower performers	2.67	27.4%	-28.6%
Turnover rates	Higher performers	3.00	37.7%	0.0%
	Lower performers	2.69	29.2%	-22.7%
Profits	Higher performers	2.78	35.5%	0.0%
	Lower performers	2.01	21.9%	-38.4%
Employee productivity	Higher performers	2.75	33.0%	0.0%
	Lower performers	2.15	14.7%	-55.4%
Employee satisfaction surveys on talent management	Higher performers	2.57	28.3%	0.0%
	Lower performers	2.42	27.4%	-3.3%
Recruitment metrics	Higher performers	2.43	24.5%	0.0%
	Lower performers	2.10	17.7%	-27.8%

Integration Is a Challenge For All Organizations

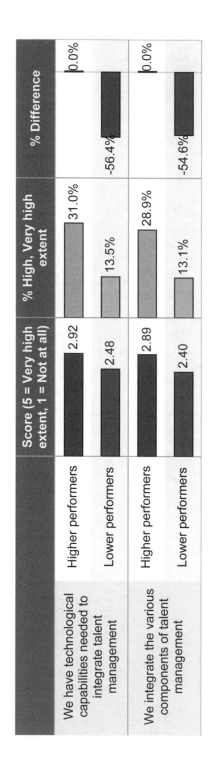

		Score (5 = Very high extent, 1 = Not at all)	% High, Very high extent	% Difference
We have technological capabilities needed to integrate talent management	Higher performers	2.92	31.0%	0.0%
	Lower performers	2.48	13.5%	-56.4%
We integrate the various components of talent management	Higher performers	2.89	28.9%	0.0%
	Lower performers	2.40	13.1%	-54.6%

Higher performing organizations report greater alignment, budget & infrastructure in place

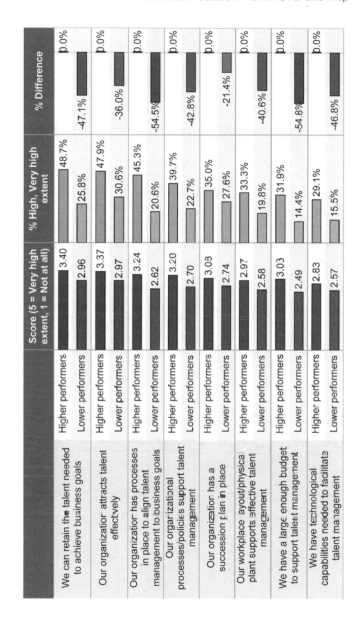

		Score (5 = Very high extent, 1 = Not at all)	% High, Very high extent	% Difference
We can retain the talent needed to achieve business goals	Higher performers	3.40	48.7%	0.0%
	Lower performers	2.96	25.8%	-47.1%
Our organization attracts talent effectively	Higher performers	3.37	47.9%	0.0%
	Lower performers	2.97	30.6%	-36.0%
Our organization has processes in place to align talent management to business goals	Higher performers	3.24	45.3%	0.0%
	Lower performers	2.62	20.6%	-54.5%
Our organizational processes/policies support talent management	Higher performers	3.20	39.7%	0.0%
	Lower performers	2.70	22.7%	-42.8%
Our organization has a succession plan in place	Higher performers	3.03	35.0%	0.0%
	Lower performers	2.74	27.6%	-21.4%
Our workplace layout/physical plant supports effective talent management	Higher performers	2.97	33.3%	0.0%
	Lower performers	2.58	19.8%	-40.6%
We have a large enough budget to support talent management	Higher performers	3.03	31.9%	0.0%
	Lower performers	2.49	14.4%	-54.8%
We have technological capabilities needed to facilitate talent management	Higher performers	2.83	29.1%	0.0%
	Lower performers	2.57	15.5%	-46.8%

About the Editors

Kevin Oakes is the CEO and founder of the Institute for Corporate Productivity (i4cp), the world's largest private network of corporations focused on improving workforce productivity. He has been a leader in the human capital field for the past two decades and was most recently the president of SumTotal Systems, a large provider of talent and learning solutions, which he founded in 2003 by merging Click2learn with Docent. Before the formation of SumTotal, he was the chairman and CEO of Click2learn. Previously, he was president and founder of Oakes Interactive, an award-winning technology-based training company. He is a frequent author and international keynote speaker on talent management and using human capital strategically in organizations.

Pat Galagan is executive editor at ASTD, responsible for covering trends in the training industry. She writes a quarterly column for *T+D* magazine and is co-author of a series of interviews with Fortune CEOs. For many years, she directed ASTD's periodicals publishing unit, launching *Learning Circuits* and *Learning Executive* magazines, and serving as editor of *T+D*.

Index